PAULA REGO

Jane Eyre

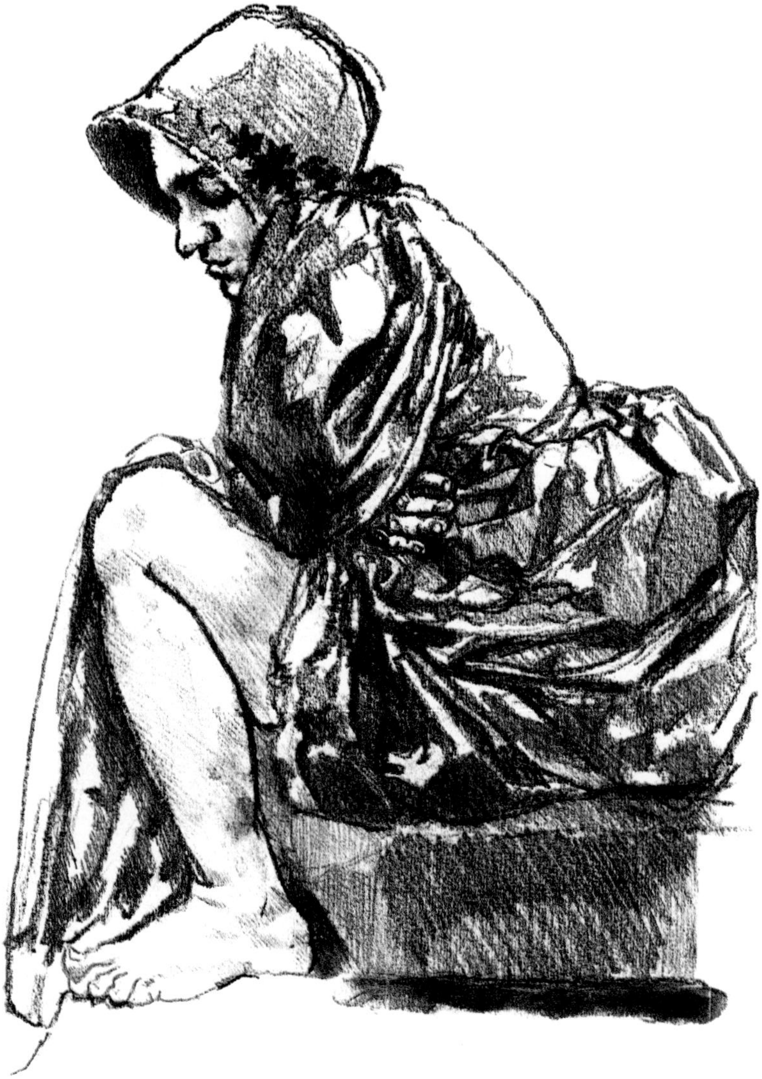

PAULA REGO

Jane Eyre

INTRODUCED BY MARINA WARNER

ENITHARMON EDITIONS LONDON
in association with
CAVALO DE FERRO EDITORES LISBON

First published in 2003
by Stephen Stuart-Smith
Enitharmon Editions Ltd
26B Caversham Road
London NW5 2DU

Trade edition issued in 2004
in association with
Cavalo de Ferro editores
Travessa dos Fiéis de Deus, 113
1200-188 Lisbon, Portugal

Images © Paula Rego 2003
Introduction © Marina Warner 2003

ISBN 1 904634 13 3 (Enitharmon Editions)
ISBN 972 8791 50 X (Cavalo de Ferro)

Note on the text:
Extracts are from Charlotte Brontë's *Jane Eyre*,
and appear in the following chapters:

1: Girl Reading at Window; Loving Bewick
2: Crumpled   6: Schoolroom
7: Refectory; Inspection   9: Jane and Helen
11: In the Comfort of the Bonnet; Jane Eyre; La Ligue des Rats
12: Mr Rochester   14: Adèle Dancing
17: Getting Ready for the Ball; Self Portrait with Grandchildren
18: Dressing him up as Bluebeard   20: Biting
25: Up the Tree   26: Crying
27: Bertha; The Keeper; Undressing; Night   35: Come to Me

The frontispiece reproduces *Jane*,
the lithograph accompanying the *de luxe* edition.

Printed in Italy

CONTENTS

INTRODUCTION	7
Girl Reading at Window	18
Loving Bewick	20
Crumpled	22
Schoolroom	24
Refectory	26
Inspection	28
Jane and Helen	30
In the Comfort of the Bonnet	32
Jane Eyre	34
La Ligue des Rats	36
Mr Rochester	38
Adèle Dancing	40
Getting Ready for the Ball	43
Self Portrait with Grandchildren	44
Dressing him up as Bluebeard	46
Biting	48
Up the Tree	50
Crying	52
Bertha	54
The Keeper	56
Undressing	58
Night	60
Come to Me	62

An artist's dreamland:
Jane Eyre through Paula Rego's eyes

MARINA WARNER

THE PROHIBITION THAT Psyche breaks, when she lights a lamp and looks on the sleeping form of her lover beside her, can only belong in a poetic order of reality. In the depths of the night, is it ever so pitch dark that she could not tell a cannibal beast of hideous aspect from the delightful youth, all golden and curly, who appears in the glow of her forbidden lamp? Even discounting her other senses – of touch above all – she would have glimpsed something of her mysterious husband. The darkness must rather be hers, from the innermost recesses of her fantasy, which have been filled with shadows by her sisters' malicious talk about the nature of her bridegroom: they have warned her that he must be hiding from her because he is a monster ready to devour her. Psyche is in the dark about her own story, and her worst suspicions and fears about her fate have been murkily stirred.

When she illuminates the scene at that fateful moment and the drop of oil falls from the lamp onto Cupid's shoulder and wakes him, everything around her vanishes, the gorgeous castle, the fairy attendants and magical banquets and concerts and apparel and diversions and visual enchantments. Her previous blindness as to her beloved's identity had opened another eye, the interior eye of fantasy, and, in every respect in her existence with Cupid, she was living in a dream world.

The story of 'Cupid and Psyche' appears within the frame of Apuleius's initiatory romance, *Metamorphosis or The Golden Ass*, and Charlotte Brontë read it in translation in *Blackwood's Magazine*, which was avidly read during the 1820s and 1830s by the whole Brontë family. The tale suffuses later fairy tales – 'Beauty and the Beast' above all – and their multiple affinities to *Jane Eyre* have often been noted, for Charlotte Brontë frequently invokes the canon of classical and nursery romances ('Bluebeard' perhaps more even than 'Cinderella'). Even the blindness of Mr Rochester at the conclusion of the novel casts him, it has been proposed, as the blind god of love. But these narrative links of motifs and plot elements do not close quite so tightly with the true sympathy between *Jane Eyre* and fairy tales that Charlotte Brontë kindles at the core of her book; this sympathy leaps up out of the persistent liveliness of interior mindscapes, in contrast to the dark, dreary, crushing realities around her heroine. Just as Psyche's existence is brilliantly illuminated in the dark of her own dream world, before she comes down to earth (literally) after lighting the lamp, so Jane Eyre is taken out of herself into a more vivid, meaningful life by her interior thoughts, through her own reading as well as the stories, which she remembers Bessie Leaven telling her, through the paintings she makes herself – all her various different stratagems of retreat from her outer circumstances. *Jane Eyre* is possibly the earliest novel written in the first person of a child: Jane is a little girl of ten years old when the book opens. But it is also a novel that, written in the confessional narrative manner, tells what occurs outside through the emotional and fantastic voyaging of its heroine's imagination. From its first appearance, the critic G. H. Lewes commented on this 'strange power of subjective representation': 'it is soul speaking to soul; it is an utterance from the depths of a struggling, suffering, much-enduring spirit: *suspiria de profundis!*'[1] The writer Angela Carter, herself a novelist in direct line of descent from the Brontës, summed up Charlotte's procedure perceptively in an introduction to the novel: '*Jane Eyre* is a peculiarly unsettling blend of penetrating psychological realism, of violent and intuitive feminism, of a surprisingly firm sociological grasp, and of the utterly non-realistic apparatus of psycho-sexual fantasy – irresistible passion, madness, violent death, dream, telepathic communication.'[2]

Again and again in the story, Jane Eyre is closeted in a small, confined space, sometimes most terribly against her will, sometimes secluded of her own accord: in an early piece of powerful scene-setting, she is locked in the dark chamber where John Reed died and is so terrified by the dead man's presence that she has a fit. This is only the first of a sequence of experiences when for better or worse imagination takes over Jane's being.

Such an emphasis on the fire in the mind and the dark outside might perhaps reveal, without saying much more, how Paula Rego of all artists would respond to *Jane Eyre*. Paula Rego has been making images out of made-up stories since she herself was a child, and if anything can be said to offer a consistent thread through her astonishing, fertile and multi-faceted production it is this: she has been a narrative artist all along, and one whose stories are not reproduced from life as observed or remembered, but from goings-on in the *camera lucida* of the mind's eye. Rego has not lost in adulthood the energy of the child's make-believe world: 'It all comes out of my head,' she says, 'All little girls improvise, and it's not just illustration: I make it my own.'

The spinal cord that runs through Rego's œuvre paradoxically joins intense looking out with even more intense looking in. Over the last decade, often working from life models, she has developed a powerful, concentrated realist technique in draughtsmanship and paint: to render the texture and play of folds of dress and fabric, the gnarled feet and wrung hands, the lined, even seamed countenances of her characters, and the dynamics of their conversation, interlacings, blows, and exchanges. But all this absorption in what goes on in the world of three dimensions and real people serves extreme acts of visual imagination, sometimes altogether impossible to enact in any other dimension: the extraordinary image *Loving Bewick*, for example, when Jane kisses the pelican's beak with an expression of eucharistic rapture. The composition recalls the picture of *Baa baa black sheep* from *Nursery Rhymes*, in which a giant ram embraces a little girl, and it also harks back to a Renaissance Leda. Paula Rego says that she became interested, when reading the novel, in the paintings that Jane Eyre herself makes and looks at, and *Loving Bewick* interprets the passage at the very start of the book when Jane describes how she loses herself in 'Bewick's *History of British Birds*', and travels through its pages to 'the solitary rocks and promontories', 'those forlorn regions of dreary space', and 'death-white realms' haunted by the book's subjects:

> Each picture told a story; mysterious often to my undeveloped understanding and imperfect feelings, yet ever profoundly

interesting: as interesting as the tales Bessie sometimes narrated on winter evenings ... and when, having brought her ironing-table to the nursery-hearth, she allowed us to sit about it, and ... fed our eager attention with passages of love and adventure taken from old fairy tales and other ballads...

With Bewick on my knee, I was then happy: happy at least in my way.[3]

In the print of Jane Eyre billing the pelican's beak, Rego has introduced a note of true sustenance: it is through the mind food offered by books and pictures that Jane Eyre survives.

In the novel, this scene of quiet, successful escapism is rudely interrupted by the bully boy John Reed, junior, who hauls Jane out from behind the curtain of the window seat, and hits her first with his hand, and then, later, forbidding her to take the family's books to read, throws the volume at her so hard that she falls to the ground. It is then that she is locked into the red-room as a punishment.

Charlotte Brontë and Paula Rego share an imaginative ardour that abolishes the veil between what takes place in fact or in fantasy. As storytellers, they really are kith and kin: Rego reproduces the psychological drama in the book through subjective distortions of scale, cruel expressiveness of gesture and frown, and disturbingly stark contrasts of light and welling shadows. The long, lugubrious, moralising face of Mr Brocklehurst, in her image of *The Inspection*, looms as large as the little girl's whole upper body and twice its bulk: Jane standing on the stool, held up by Bessie, becomes a tiny, breakable poppet. Similarly, in *The Schoolroom*, her vulnerability shapes her tiny size, while her classmates, like Goya's *Caprichos*, form a chorus of powerless, grimacing watchers like so many monsters of the dream of reason. Rego shows Jane from the back (three times) and with her eyes turned away or closed (eight times) to propel us, the readers turned viewers, into entering into her interior life (portraits designed to display the external features of a subject have their eyes wide open, looking out).

Jane Eyre's own paintings also inspired Paula Rego, just as, in the novel, they interest Mr Rochester. He looks at her portfolio and, later, he shows them round to his friends. They give him an insight into the originality of her character, and they introduce him to her passionate strength of mind. The first encounter between them takes place when Jane comes across Rochester on his horse and helps him after his fall; that 'incident of no moment' breaks into her monotonous life', but a deeper exchange between them arises afterwards, from his perusal of her portfolio. He asks, 'I perceive these pictures were done by one hand: was that hand yours?'

'Yes.'

…

'Where did you get your copies?'
'Out of my head.'
'That head I see now on your shoulders?'
'Yes, sir.'
'Has it other furniture of the same kind within?'[4]

The dialogue catches faultlessly the mixture of condescension and gallantry in an older man's approach to a young woman's work when he finds himself taken by surprise at its interest. Jane herself does not vaunt her work ('they are nothing wonderful') but she does repeat, 'The subjects had indeed risen vividly on my mind. As I saw them with the spiritual eye, before I attempted to embody them, they were striking; but my hand would not second my fancy…'[5] It could be Paula Rego talking, if one sets aside that last reservation, for indeed her mind has furniture of the same kind within.

Jane Eyre's medium is watercolour, and her subjects seem to have floated out of a Coleridgian poem: a shipwreck with a drowned woman, whose gold bracelet has been stolen by a cormorant; a vision of the Evening Star personified, whose 'eyes shone dark and wild', and the spectacle of the Northern Lights as a kind of colossal spectre, 'white as bone'. In the lithograph *Night*, Paula Rego echoes the second of these visions, in the form of a portrait of Jane, looking out as if in pain and fear from the folds of her dress, pulled over her head for shelter on that terrible night when, stripped of everything, she leaves Thornfield Hall.

'"I daresay," says Mr Rochester, "You did exist in a kind of artist's dreamland while you blent and arranged these strange tints."'[6] Later, he returns to the theme, '"...the drawings are, for a school girl, peculiar. As to the thoughts, they are elfish."'[6]

In Paula Rego's work, in her 'artist's dreamland', the peculiar and the elfish twist and turn with a similar rebellious vitality. And they do so for reasons that Jane Eyre's did, mirroring Charlotte Brontë's, over a hundred and fifty years ago. Rego has explored, in a myriad different sequences of pictures, the conditions of her own upbringing in Portugal, her formation as a girl and a woman, and the oscillation between stifling social expectations and liberating female stratagems.

II

AT ONE POINT Jane Eyre protests, 'Women are supposed to be very calm generally: but women feel just as men feel; they need exercise for their faculties, and a field for their efforts as much as their brothers do; they suffer from too rigid a restraint, too absolute a stagnation, precisely as men would suffer; and it is narrow-minded in their more privileged fellow-creatures to say that they ought to confine themselves to making puddings and knitting stockings, to playing on the piano and embroidering bags...'[7] In her brilliantly observed later novel, *Shirley*, Charlotte Brontë develops this theme with even more ardent partisanship, especially in a masterly chapter, 'Old Maids', which looks with tenderness, wit and fighting spirit at the lives of impoverished, philanthropic gentlefolk.[8] It shows just how deeply Brontë could imagine herself into the littlest lives, of women who could not say, at the end of the book, 'Reader, I married him.'

In *Jane Eyre*, her outburst on women's lot segues without any obvious link to a new paragraph, which begins: 'When thus alone, I not unfrequently heard Grace Poole's laugh...' Jane still does not know at this stage that Grace Poole is not the source of the disturbing cries and cackling she hears; she learns of the existence of Bertha Mason later. But by introducing the woman confined and invisible (the madwoman in the attic) in counterpoint to Jane's thoughts about the constrictions on a woman's life, Charlotte Brontë suggests to the reader that Mr Rochester's crazy Creole wife represents a terrible example of what can happen to a woman in the bond of marriage. Bertha is Jane's potential shadow double, the embodiment of a possible ghastly fate, and figures in the novel like the ghoulish cautionary tale Mr Brocklehurst thrusts at Jane, ordering her to: '...read it with prayer, especially that part containing "an account of the awfully sudden death of Martha G——, a naughty child addicted to falsehood and deceit."'[9]

Brontë shows little compassion for Bertha Mason, but rather communicates profound horror at her degradation, in the same way as in *Villette* she also depicts Lucy Snowe recoiling from the 'cretin' who terrifies her in the *pension*. But unconsciously, Brontë strikes the reader as taking such matters personally, repudiating what she most fears will be the outcome of a narrow, suffocating, oppressive, loveless and directionless life.

Paula Rego's portrayals of Jane do not prettify her, as have done most of the jacket illustrations and films over the years, but remain faithful to the novel's insistence on her plainness of feature, that makes her 'such a little toad' in the eyes of the bitter lady's maid, Abbott;[10] in so doing, in depicting Jane as neither slender nor graceful nor even *jolie-laide*, Rego closes the distance between Jane Eyre and Bertha Mason, and illuminates the fate they could share, if Jane did not use her strength and originality of character to withstand society's sentence on genteel women. The moods Rego has selected to dramatise show Jane stricken with melancholy (*In the Comfort of the Bonnet*), flung face down on the floor in grief (*Crumpled*) and grimacing with longing (*Come to Me*): the physicality of Jane's body matches here the animal groundedness of Rego's Bertha.

Girlhood and its appetites have inspired Paula Rego's picture-making for over thirty years, and her works in this vein include the brilliantly fluent and mischievous sequence of paintings *The Vivian Girls*, inspired by Henry Darger's extraordinary, epic scroll novel, populated by heroines, part Enid Blyton schoolgirls, part Surrealist *femmes-enfants*. Furiously intent young women, capricious, cruel, wilful in their confined domesticity, attend to one another or to animals or to daily, banal tasks; the scenes Paula Rego summons up dramatise the limits on female expectation imposed on Rego in her youth. For although she comes from a liberal family, and was sent by her father to an English school, the equivalent of the French lycée, she was still steeped in the culture of Salazar's dictatorship, founded on the Catholic church, the army, and the idealisation of Woman as wife and mother – and servant. The perverted uses of female power, when squeezed behind the scenes or into the sewing room and the kitchen, erupt in Rego's imagery with seemingly irrepressible force; she brims over with the same keen, impassioned sense of its malignity as Charlotte Brontë does in her creation of Bertha Mason.

III

TO COMMUNICATE DREAM WORLDS on the one hand, and to interfuse them with social critique on the other, Paula Rego has found the medium of print supremely apt, in its spontaneity of execution, and its long relation to storytelling. She has long defied prejudice against narrative painting, and has reclaimed illustrated tales for grown-up readers. She has absorbed with enthusiasm the dramatic expressiveness of the European graphic illustrators such as Max Klinger, Gustave Doré, Gavarni, Steinlem and Cham, who were working for the new weekly and monthly picture press in the late nineteenth century. These have shaped her book illustration far more than the ornamental, fairy tale specialists, Arthur Rackham and Edmond Dulac. The commercial arts of fashion, advertising, the boulevard, the new department stores and the reportage on *faits divers* in nineteenth-century modernity claim as their own the traditions of sacred drama, seizing on the crucial moment, the climactic encounter, as in a Guercino drawing or an Orazio Gentileschi painting (both skilled at narrative gesture, and artists she loves). Some of the impact of Rego's masterly draughtsmanship arises from highly personal marks made by lithographic crayons on stone; she exults in the sticky softness of the medium, which 'really shows up the drawing', and she praises the methods her printer Stanley Jones has perfected over the years to produce sensitive pulls. Her sumptuous image of Jane Eyre from the back displays Rego's virtuoso skills: the play of light in the cloth, the contrast of shadows moulding her head and body with the recessive darkness towards which she is moving, form a perfectly attuned rendering of the heroine's isolation, desperation and –

determination to resist. She recalls the moodiness of Plath's lines about the moon: 'staring from her hood of bone … Her blacks crackle and drag.'

When I was first reading the heady fictions of Conan Doyle and Rider Haggard, they came with illustrations, in the copies of the *Strand Magazine* my father had, and in the editions of *She* or *King Solomon's Mines* issued for both children and adults in the Fifties. The pictures made a point, or even, to follow the concept Roland Barthes uses in his book on photography, a *punctum*: singling out a moment, they pierced through the veil of words and materialised a kind of essence of story. I shall never forget the thrill of the image, under which was written: 'It was the footsteps of a gigantic hound' (although now, I feel, Conan Doyle cannot have written footsteps, but something like marks or tracks, surely.) Flicking through volumes that I still have from those years, I see that the artists used acute angles, raked perspectives, plunging viewpoints to accentuate the drama, which the captions intensified even more: 'Another Secret Passage', 'A Queer Discovery'.

Picture books for children today do not serve to heighten or punctuate the text: image and word combine and flow, like voices in a duet. Rego's responses to a classic tale of mythical aura, like *Jane Eyre*, translate the novel's character into another medium, reproducing its mood and its texture in kinetic line and moulding shadows. The benightedness of Jane Eyre's state finds its correlative in the inkiness from which she materialises before our eyes; the dynamic nature of her resistance to her fate leaps in the vitality of her contours, and so forth: the visual technique matches narrative wordplay in reciprocal counterpoint. In a recent study of mental picturing, *Dreaming by the Book*, the American critic Elaine Scarry offers some highly original insights into the relationship between daydreaming, reading, and visualising, which throw light on the work of an artist like Paula Rego. She draws attention to the intrinsically dreamy properties of some phenomena, such as gauze or clouds or rain, which align them with objects of reverie which cannot be summoned up in their solid substance by the mind's eye. 'We might say', she writes, that in fog the physical universe approaches the condition of the imagination'.[11] Later, she adds, 'It is not hard to imagine a ghost successfully. What is hard is successfully to imagine an object, any object, that does *not* look like a ghost.'[12]

It is this weakness of imaginative projection, for most of us, that lends such power to the technical media which simulate the stuff that dreams are made on: daguerreotypes, phantasmagoria, lantern slides, and film replicate the thinness, spectrality, and fugitive aspects of conscious, mental acts of visualisation.[13] These comments on cognitive capacity offer a context for thinking about Rego and about the distinctive principles of book illustration, for what she achieves is precisely that solidity, that density of presence, that stable durability that usually elude the mind's eye of the reader. But – and this but is a most important modifier – her images do not realise Jane Eyre or other figures as in the literal enactments of contemporary full colour cinema: they retain dreamlike qualities. In the typical realist television adaptation, there are so many historic locations and vehicles, props and costumes, such heaps of furniture and whole archives of ornaments. But drawing out of the mind straight on to the plate or the stone does not need the half of all that paraphernalia: in its grasp of mood and atmosphere, of the dream feeling, just a minimum of external detail is necessary.

Scarry also argues that 'The vibrancy of perception – the rush of colour, the spill of light, the thrilling density or discontinuity of sound – is less likely to be duplicated during undirected daydreaming than when dreaming-by-the-book. Our freely practiced imaginative acts bear less resemblance to our freely practiced perceptual acts than do our constrained imaginative acts occurring under authorial direction.'[14] This is a rather convoluted way of saying that Brontë makes us see things more sharply than we could manage without her, and that writing vividly is often about that assistance to the reader; Paula Rego, it seems to me, performs the mediating task of imagining elements of the story with fidelity to its dreamlike – even nightmarish – qualities, and yet, as I said, enfleshing them at the same time in an elusive real-life, grounded thickness of experience. In this too, Rego retains to a quite extraordinary degree the brilliant imperiousness of childhood consciousness that calls into being all its imaginings: 'the very young child,' wrote Jean-Paul Sartre, 'acts upon the world from his bed by orders and entreaties. The objects obey these orders of consciousness: they appear.'[15]

Paula Rego is able to record that coming-into-being of her dream world and, in her illustrations to *Jane Eyre*, as she sees with Jane's 'spiritual eye', through Charlotte Brontë's dramatic storytelling, through its heroine's trials and survival back to her personal experiences of benightedness, her work helps release her viewers from that state. She lights up a different way of seeing, as when Psyche struggles through one kind of darkness into another.

1 Quoted Lucasta Miller, *The Brontë Myth* (London, 2001), pp. 12–13.
2 Angela Carter, 'Charlotte Brontë: Jane Eyre', in *Expletives Deleted* (London, 1992), p. 161.
3 Charlotte Bronte, *Jane Eyre* [1847], chapter 1, ed. Michael Mason (London: Penguin Classics, 1996), pp. 14–15.
4 Brontë, *Jane Eyre*, chapter 13, op. cit, p. 142.
5 Brontë, *Jane Eyre*, chapter 13, op. cit., p. 142.
6 Brontë, *Jane Eyre*, chapter 13, op. cit. pp. 142–4.
7 Brontë, *Jane Eyre*, chapter 12, op. cit., pp. 125–6.
8 Charlotte Brontë, *Shirley* [1849], vol. 1, chapter x, eds. Herbert Rosengarten and Margaret Smith (Oxford, 1979), pp. 166–184.
9 Brontë, *Jane Eyre*, chapter 4, op. cit, p. 44.
10 Brontë, *Jane Eyre*, chapter 3, op. cit., p. 34.
11 Elaine Scarry, *Dreaming by the Book* (New York, 1999), p. 23.
12 Ibid., p. 24.
13 See Marina Warner, 'Spirit Visions: Faces in the Clouds, or, Figuring the Invisible', *Raritan* (Summer 2002), pp. 264–301.
14 Scarry, op. cit., p. 31.
15 Jean-Paul Sartre, *The Psychology of Imagination* (New York, 1991), p. 177, quoted Scarry, op. cit., p. 32.

Girl Reading at Window

A SMALL BREAKFAST-ROOM adjoined the drawing-room: I slipped in there. It contained a book-case: I soon possessed myself of a volume, taking care that it should be one stored with pictures. I mounted into the window-seat: gathering up my feet, I sat cross-legged, like a Turk; and, having drawn the red moreen curtain nearly close, I was shrined in double retirement.

Folds of scarlet drapery shut in my view to the right hand; to the left were the clear panes of glass, protecting, but not separating me from the drear November day. At intervals, while turning over the leaves of my book, I studied the aspect of that winter afternoon. Afar, it offered a pale blank of mist and cloud; near, a scene of wet lawn and storm-beat shrub, with ceaseless rain sweeping away wildly before a long and lamentable blast.

*

The breakfast-room door opened.

'Boh! Madam Mope!' cried the voice of John Reed; then he paused: he found the room apparently empty.

'Where the dickens is she?' he continued. 'Lizzy! Georgy!' (calling to his sisters) 'Jane is not here: tell mama she is run out into the rain – bad animal!'

'It is well I drew the curtain,' thought I; and I wished fervently he might not discover my hiding-place; nor would John Reed have found it out himself; he was not quick either of vision or conception; but Eliza just put her head in at the door, and said at once: –

'She is in the window-seat, to be sure, Jack.'

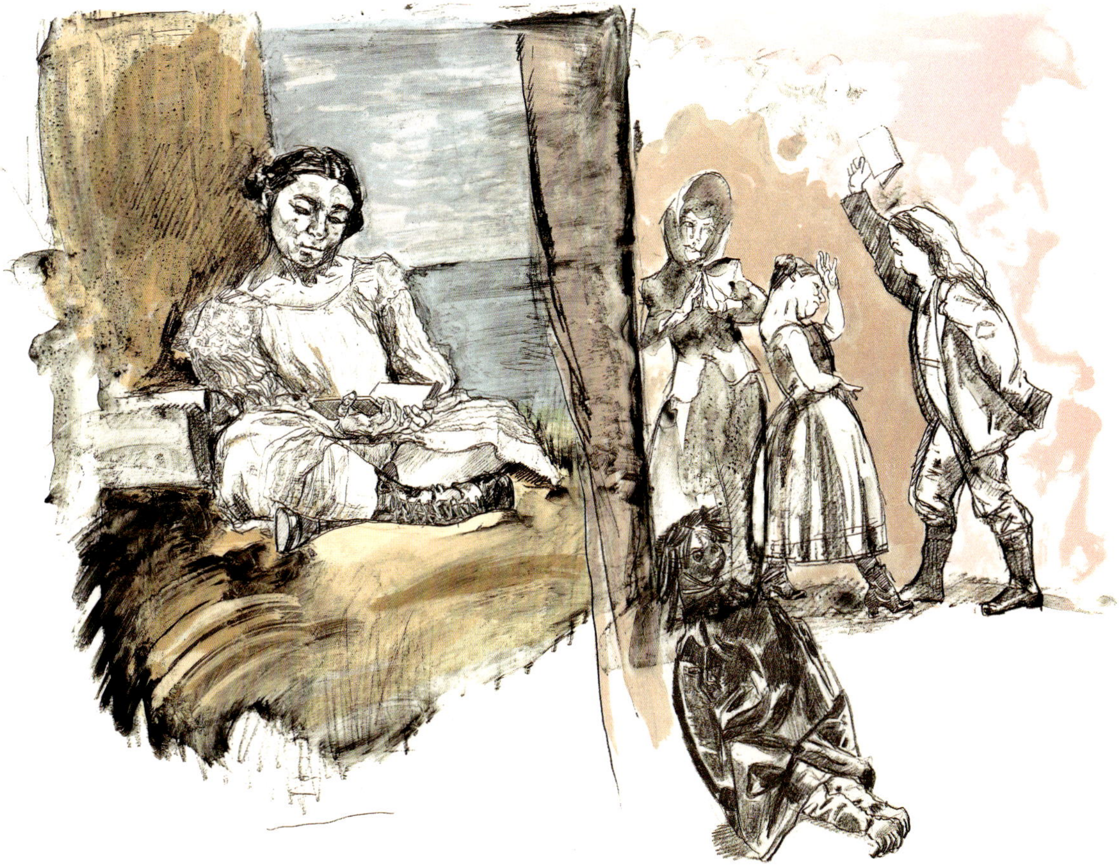

Loving Bewick

I RETURNED TO my book – Bewick's *History of British Birds*: the letter-press thereof I cared little for, generally speaking; and yet there were certain introductory pages that, child as I was, I could not pass quite as a blank. They were those which treat of the haunts of sea-fowl; of 'the solitary rocks and promontories' by them only inhabited; of the coast of Norway, studded with isles from its southern extremity, the Lindeness, or Naze, to the North Cape –

> Where the Northern Ocean, in vast whirls
> Boils round the naked, melancholy isles
> Of farthest Thule; and the Atlantic surge
> Pours in among the stormy Hebrides.

Nor could I pass unnoticed the suggestion of the bleak shores of Lapland, Siberia, Spitzbergen, Nova Zembla, Iceland, Greenland, with the vast sweep of the Arctic Zone, and those forlorn regions of dreary space, – that reservoir of frost and snow, where firm fields of ice, the accumulation of centuries of winters, glazed in Alpine heights above heights, surround the pole, and concentre the multiplied rigors of extreme cold.' Of these death-white realms I formed an idea of my own: shadowy, like all the half-comprehended notions that float dim through children's brains, but strangely impressive.

*

Each picture told a story; mysterious often to my undeveloped understanding and imperfect feelings, yet ever profoundly interesting…

*

With Bewick on my knee, I was then happy: happy at least in my way. I feared nothing but interruption, and that came too soon.

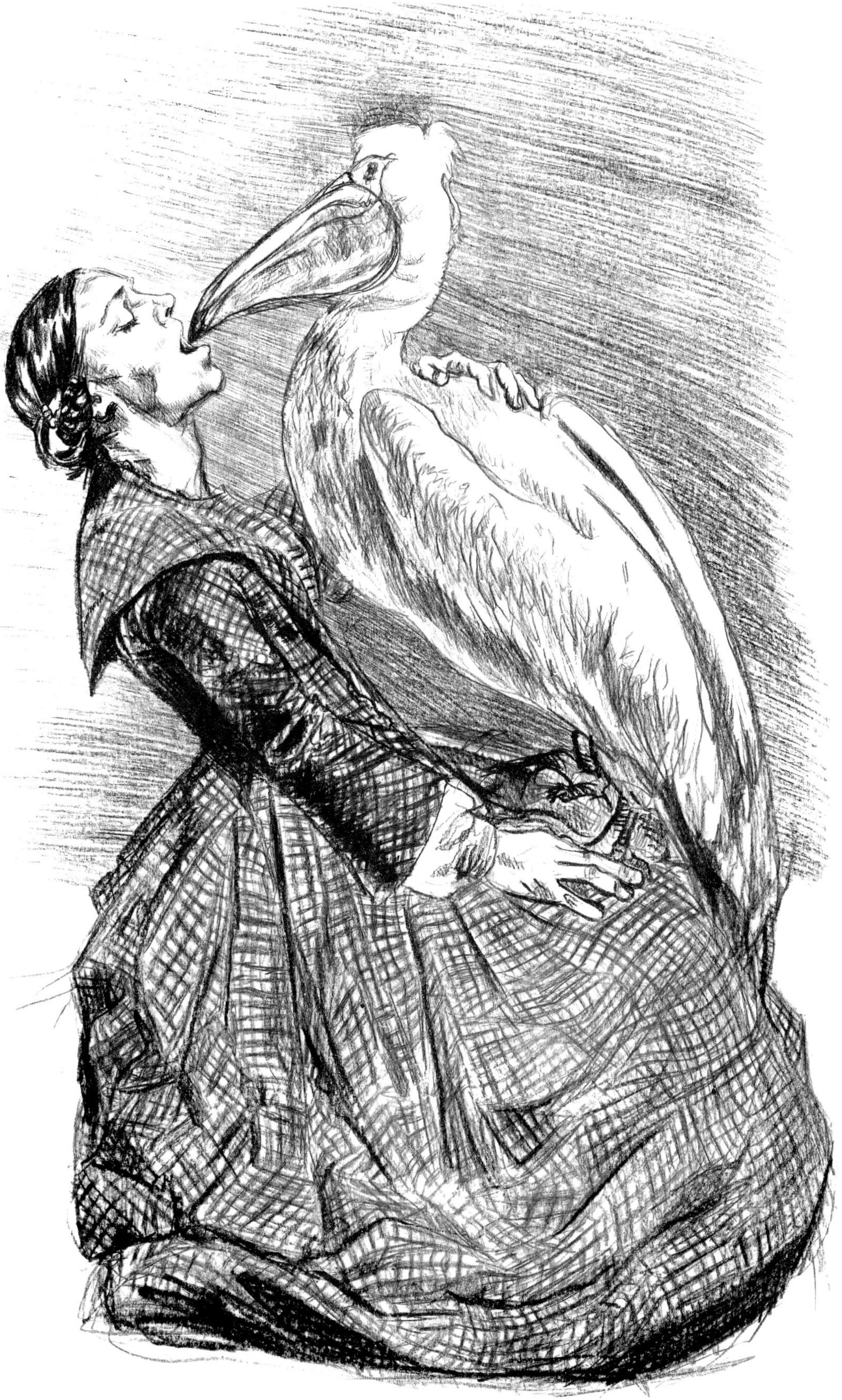

Crumpled

My heart beat thick, my head grew hot; a sound filled my ears, which I deemed the rushing of wings: something seemed near me; I was oppressed, suffocated: endurance broke down – I uttered a wild, involuntary cry – I rushed to the door and shook the lock in desperate effort.

*

'O aunt, have pity! Forgive me! I cannot endure it – let me be punished some other way! I shall be killed if –'

'Silence! This violence is all most repulsive:' and so, no doubt, she felt it. I was a precocious actress in her eyes: she sincerely looked on me as a compound of virulent passions, mean spirit, and dangerous duplicity.

Bessie and Abbot having retreated, Mrs Reed, impatient of my now frantic anguish and wild sobs, abruptly thrust me back and locked me in, without farther parley. I heard her sweeping away; and soon after she was gone, I suppose I had a species of fit: unconsciousness closed the scene.

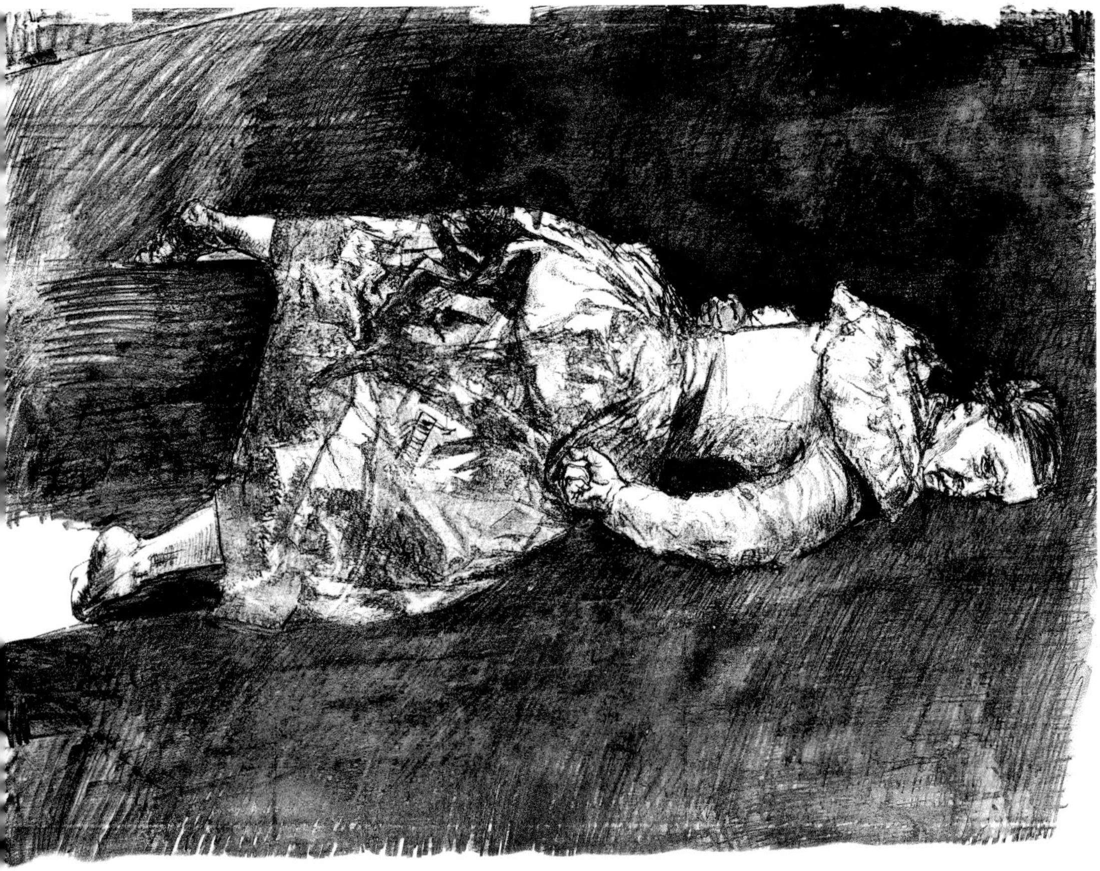

Schoolroom

WHEN I RETURNED to my seat, that lady was just delivering an order, of which I did not catch the import; but Burns immediately left the class, and, going into the small inner room where the books were kept, returned in half a minute, carrying in her hand a bundle of twigs tied together at one end. This ominous tool she presented to Miss Scatcherd with a respectful courtesy; then she quietly, and without being told, unloosed her pinafore, and the teacher instantly and sharply inflicted on her neck a dozen strokes with the bunch of twigs. Not a tear rose to Burns's eye; and, while I paused from my sewing, because my fingers quivered at this spectacle with a sentiment of unavailing and impotent anger, not a feature of her pensive face altered its ordinary expression.

'Hardened girl!' exclaimed Miss Scatcherd, 'nothing can correct you of your slatternly habits: carry the rod away.'

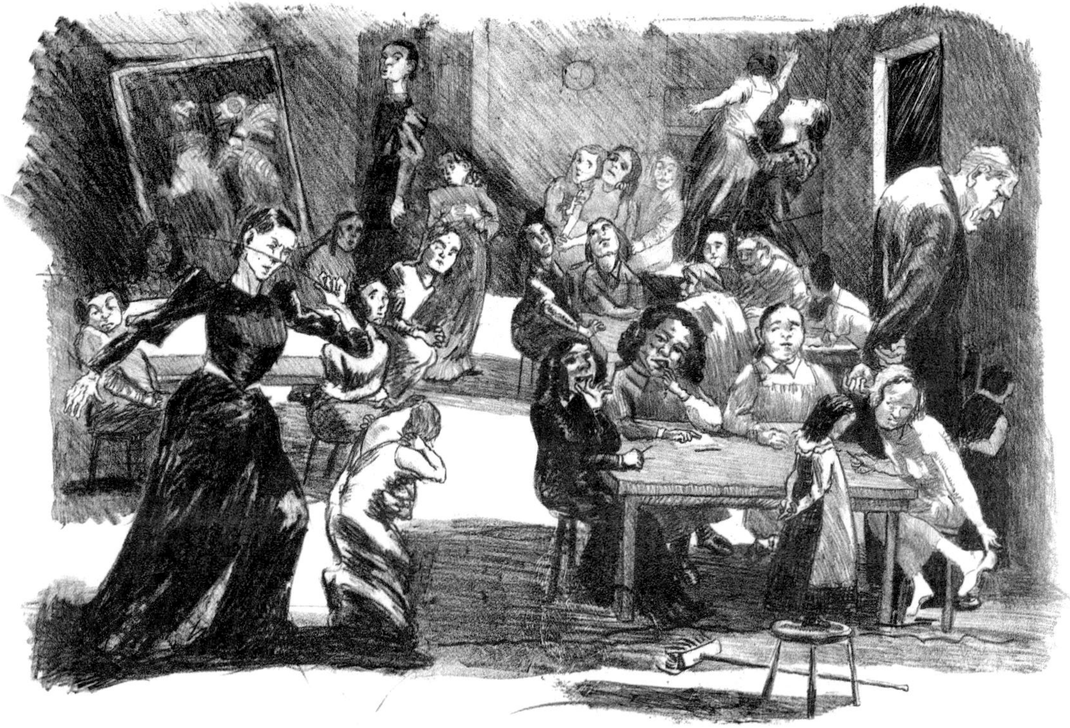

Refectory

Then the scanty supply of food was distressing: with the keen appetites of growing children, we had scarcely sufficient to keep alive a delicate invalid. From this deficiency of nourishment resulted an abuse, which pressed hardly on the younger pupils: whenever the famished great girls had an opportunity, they would coax or menace the little ones out of their portion. Many a time I have shared between two claimants the precious morsel of brown bread distributed at tea-time; and after relinquishing to a third, half the contents of my mug of coffee, I have swallowed the remainder with an accompaniment of secret tears, forced from me by the exigency of hunger.

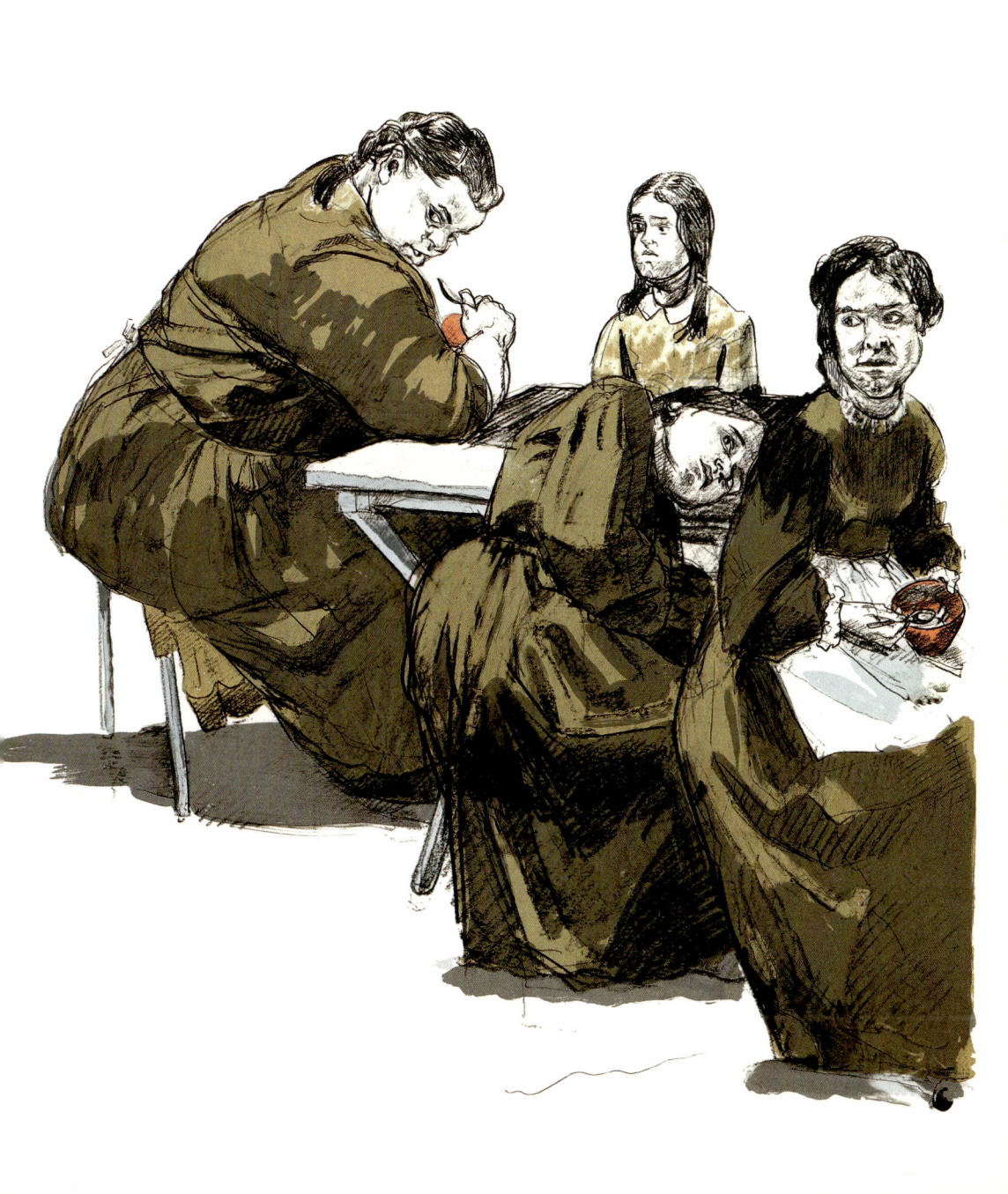

Inspection

'Fetch that stool,' said Mr Brocklehurst, pointing to a very high one from which a monitor had just risen: it was brought.

'Place the child upon it.'

And I was placed there, by whom I don't know: I was in no condition to note particulars; I was only aware that they had hoisted me up to the height of Mr Brocklehurst's nose, that he was within a yard of me, and that a spread of shot orange and purple silk pelisses, and a cloud of silvery plumage extended and waved below me.

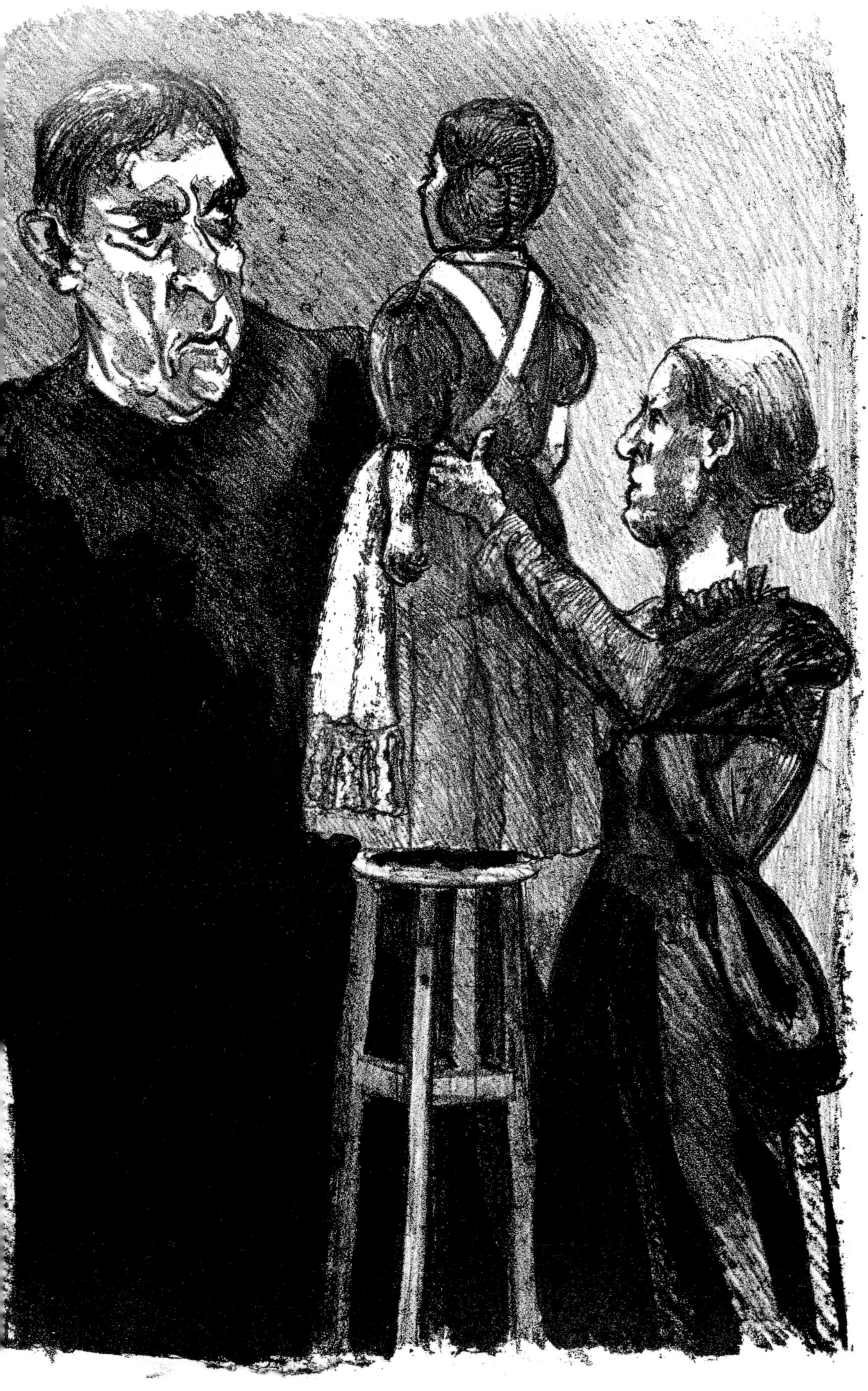

Jane and Helen

I GOT ON to her crib and kissed her: her forehead was cold, and her cheek both cold and thin, and so were her hand and wrist; but she smiled as of old.

'Why are you come here, Jane? It is past eleven o'clock: I heard it strike some minutes since.'

'I came to see you, Helen: I heard you were very ill, and I could not sleep till I had spoken to you.'

'You came to bid me good-bye, then: you are just in time probably.'

'Are you going somewhere, Helen? Are you going home?'

'Yes; to my long home – my last home.'

'No, no, Helen!' I stopped, distressed. While I tried to devour my tears, a fit of coughing seized Helen; it did not, however, wake the nurse; when it was over, she lay some minutes exhausted; then she whispered: –

'Jane, your little feet are bare; lie down and cover yourself with my quilt.'

I did so: she put her arm over me, and I nestled close to her. After a long silence, she resumed; still whispering, –

'I am very happy, Jane; and when you hear that I am dead you must be sure and not grieve: there is nothing to grieve about. We all must die one day, and the illness which is removing me is not painful; it is gentle and gradual: my mind is at rest. I leave no one to regret me much: I have only a father; and he is lately married, and will not miss me. By dying young I shall escape great sufferings. I had not qualities or talents to make my way very well in the world: I should have been continually at fault.'

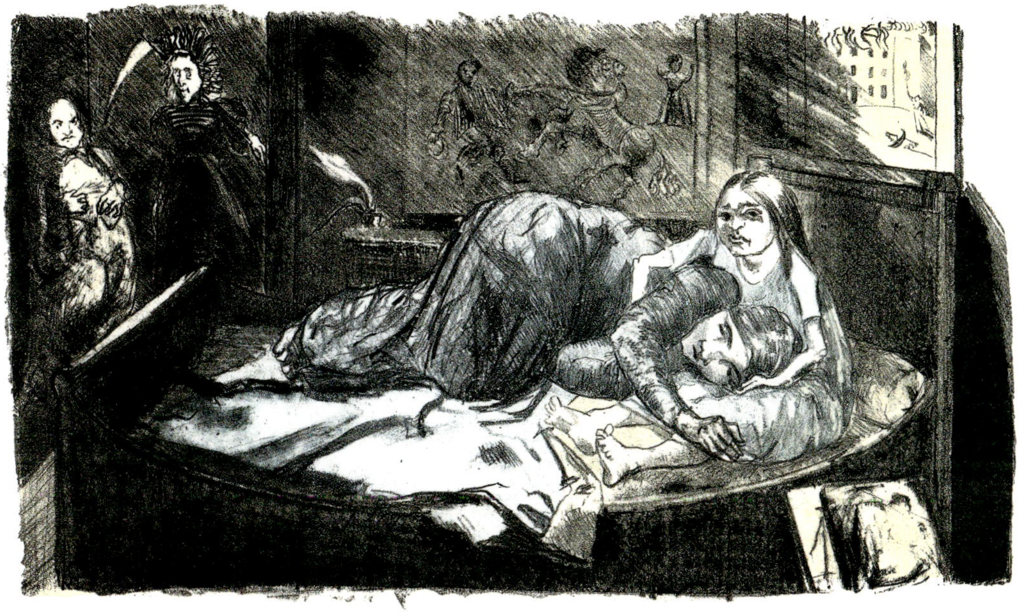

In the Comfort of the Bonnet

A NEW CHAPTER in a novel is something like a new scene in a play; and when I draw up the curtain this time, reader, you must fancy you see a room in the George Inn at Millcote, with such large figured papering on the walls as inn rooms have; such a carpet, such furniture, such ornaments on the mantel-piece, such prints; including a portrait of George the Third, and another of the Prince of Wales, and a representation of the death of Wolfe. All this is visible to you by the light of an oil-lamp hanging from the ceiling, and by that of an excellent fire, near which I sit in my cloak and bonnet; my muff and umbrella lie on the table, and I am warming away the numbness and chill contracted by sixteen hours' exposure to the rawness of an October day: I left Lowton at four o'clock p.m., and the Millcote town clock is now just striking eight.

Reader, though I look comfortably accommodated, I am not very tranquil in my mind. I thought when the coach stopped here there would be some one to meet me; I looked anxiously round as I descended the wooden steps the 'boots' placed for my convenience, expecting to hear my name pronounced, and to see some description of carriage waiting to convey me to Thornfield. Nothing of the sort was visible; and when I asked a waiter if any one had been to inquire after a Miss Eyre, I was answered in the negative: so I had no resource but to request to be shown into a private room: and here I am waiting, while all sorts of doubts and fears are troubling my thoughts.

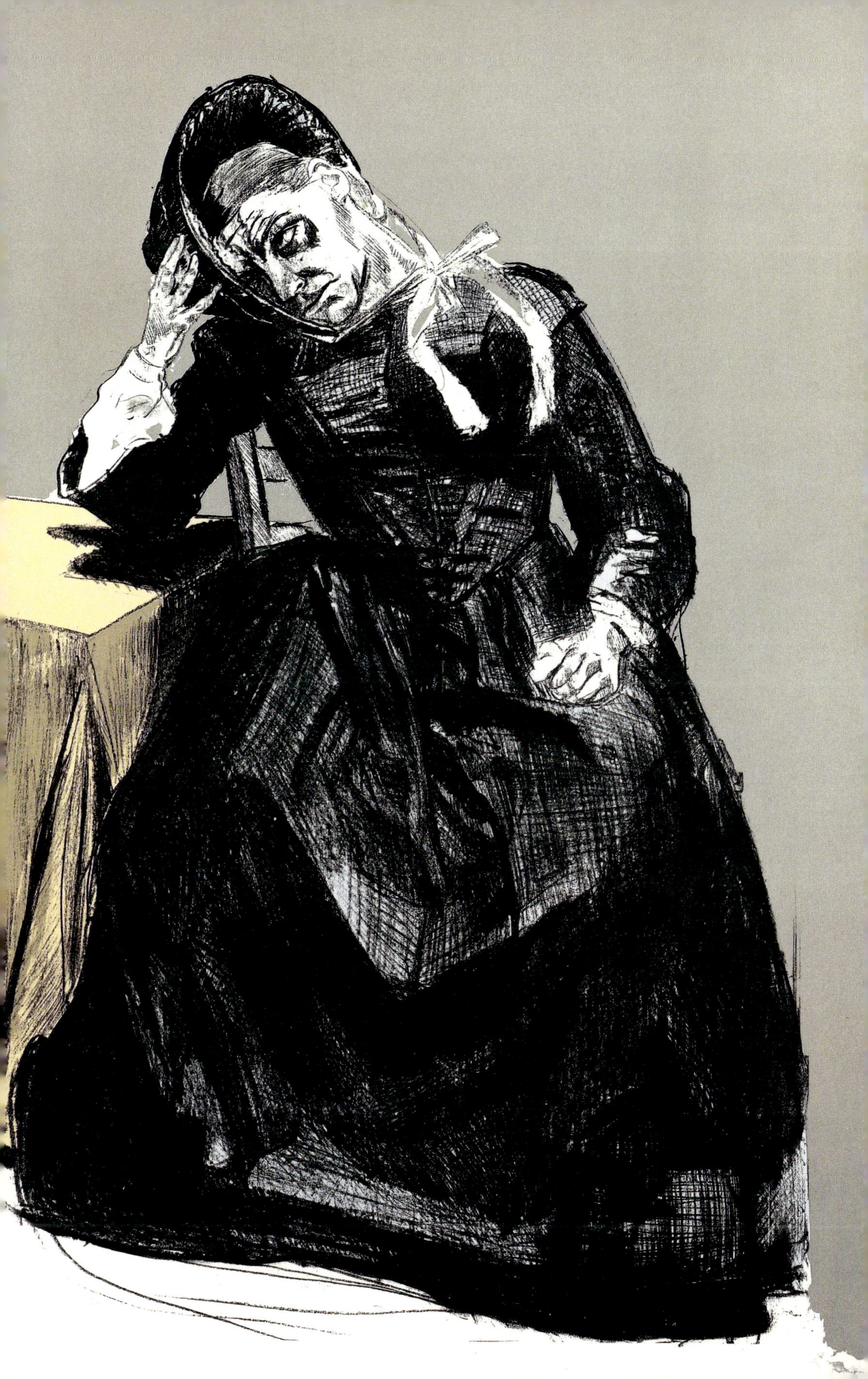

Jane Eyre

I ROSE; I dressed myself with care: obliged to be plain – for I had no article of attire that was not made with extreme simplicity – I was still by nature solicitous to be neat. It was not my habit to be disregardful of appearance, or careless of the impression I made: on the contrary, I ever wished to look as well as I could, and to please as much as my want of beauty would permit. I sometimes regretted that I was not handsomer: I sometimes wished to have rosy cheeks, a straight nose, and small cherry mouth; I desired to be tall, stately and finely developed in figure; I felt it a misfortune that I was so little, so pale, and had features so irregular and so marked. And why had I these aspirations and these regrets? It would be difficult to say: I could not then distinctly say it to myself; yet I had a reason, and a logical, natural reason too. However, when I had brushed my hair very smooth, and put on my black frock – which, Quaker-like as it was, at least had the merit of fitting to a nicety – and adjusted my clean white tucker, I thought I should do respectably enough to appear before Mrs Fairfax; and that my new pupil would not at least recoil from me with antipathy. Having opened my chamber window, and seen that I left all things straight and neat on the toilet table, I ventured forth.

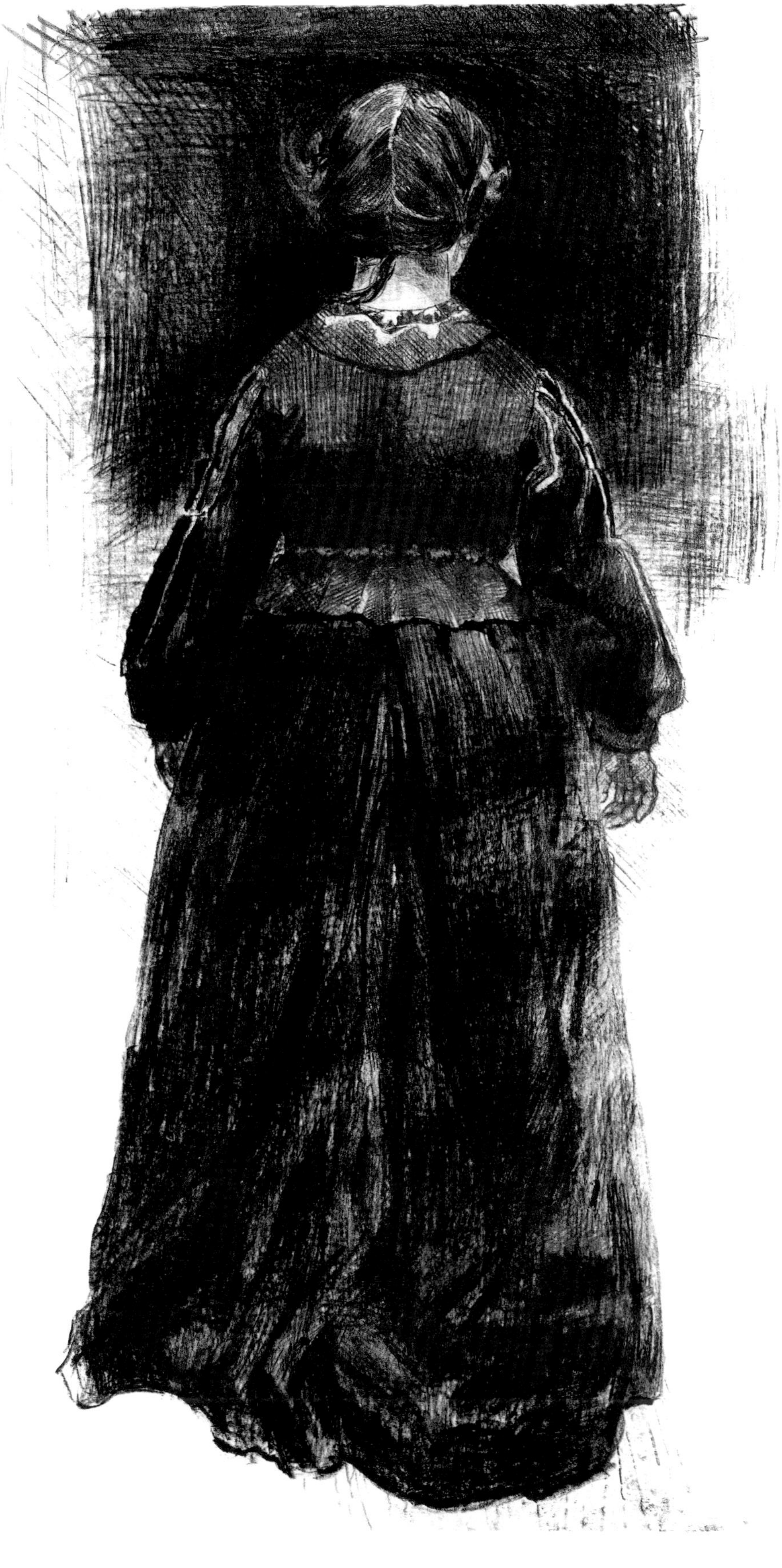

La Ligue des Rats

'I LIVED LONG AGO with mama; but she is gone to the Holy Virgin. Mama used to teach me to dance and sing, and to say verses. A great many gentlemen and ladies came to see mama, and I used to dance before them, or to sit on their knees and sing to them: I liked it. Shall I let you hear me sing now?'

She had finished her breakfast, so I permitted her to give a specimen of her accomplishments. Descending from her chair, she came and placed herself on my knee; then, folding her little hands demurely before her, shaking back her curls and lifting her eyes to the ceiling, she commenced singing a song from some opera. It was the strain of a forsaken lady, who, after bewailing the perfidy of her lover, calls pride to her aid; desires her attendant to deck her in her brightest jewels and richest robes, and resolves to meet the false one that night at a ball, and prove to him by the gaiety of her demeanour how little his desertion has affected her.

The subject seemed strangely chosen for an infant singer; but I suppose the point of the exhibition lay in hearing the notes of love and jealousy warbled with the lisp of childhood; and in very bad taste that point was: at least I thought so.

Adèle sang the canzonette tunefully enough, and with the naïveté of her age. This achieved, she jumped from my knee and said, 'Now, Mademoiselle, I will repeat you some poetry.'

Assuming an attitude, she began 'La Ligue des Rats; fable de La Fontaine.' She then declaimed the little piece with an attention to punctuation and emphasis, a flexibility of voice and an appropriateness of gesture, very unusual indeed at her age; and which proved she had been carefully trained.

'Was it your mama who taught you that piece?' I asked.

'Yes, and she just used to say it in this way: "Qu'avez vous donc? lui dit un de ces rats; parlez!" She made me lift my hand – so – to remind me to raise my voice at the question. Now shall I dance for you?'

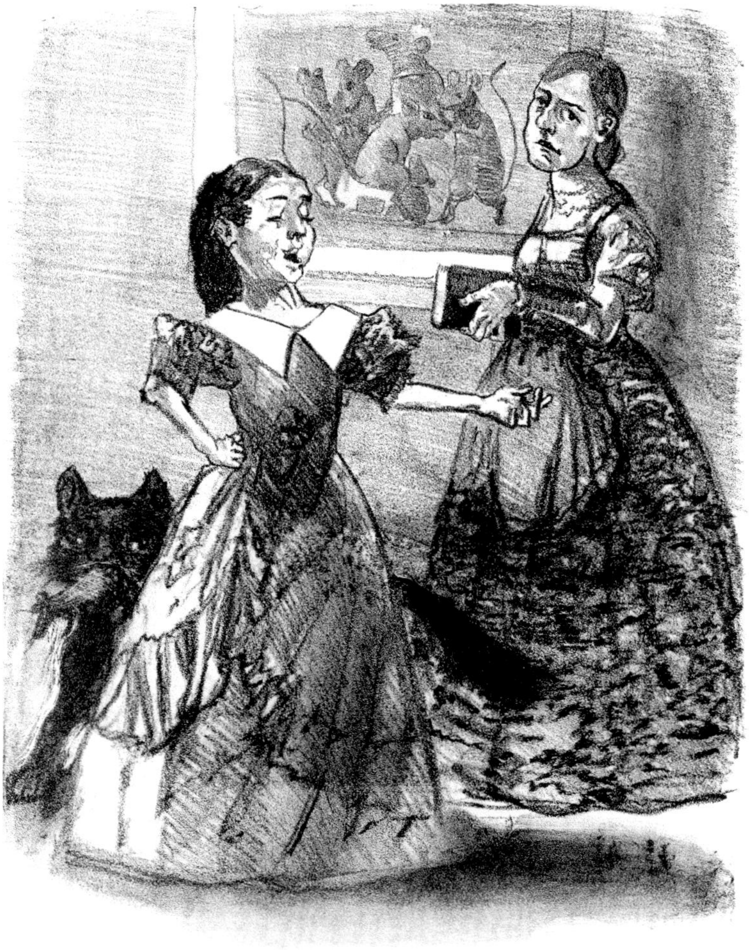

Mr Rochester

SOMETHING OF DAYLIGHT still lingered, and the moon was waxing bright: I could see him plainly. His figure was enveloped in a riding cloak, fur collared, and steel clasped; its details were not apparent, but I traced the general points of middle height, and considerable breadth of chest. He had a dark face, with stern features and a heavy brow; his eyes and gathered eyebrows looked ireful and thwarted just now; he was past youth, but had not reached middle age; perhaps he might be thirty-five. I felt no fear of him, and but little shyness.

*

Having once caught the bridle, he mastered it directly, and sprang to his saddle; grimacing grimly as he made the effort, for it wrenched his sprain.

'Now,' said he, releasing his under lip from a hard bite, 'just hand me my whip; it lies there under the hedge.'

I sought it and found it.

'Thank you; now make haste with the letter to Hay, and return as fast as you can.'

A touch of a spurred heel made his horse first start and rear, and then bound away; the dog rushed in his traces: all three vanished

> Like heath that in the wilderness
> The wild wind whirls away.

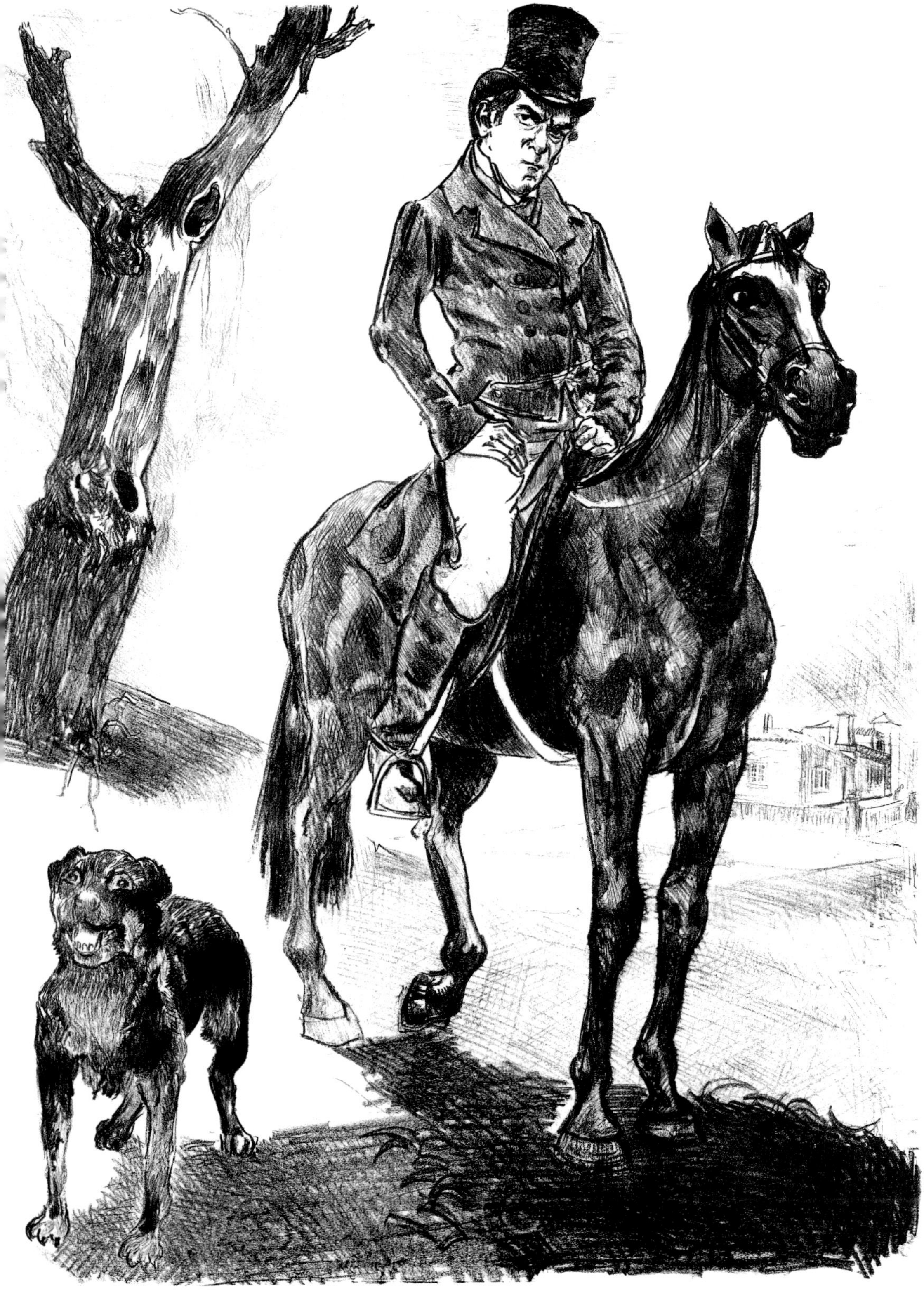

Adèle Dancing

Ere long, adèle's little foot was heard tripping across the hall. She entered, transformed as her guardian had predicted. A dress of rose-coloured satin, very short, and as full in the skirt as it could be gathered, replaced the brown frock she had previously worn; a wreath of rosebuds circled her forehead; her feet were dressed in silk stockings and small white satin sandals.

'Est-ce que ma robe va bien?' cried she, bounding forwards; 'et mes souliers? et mes bas? Tenez, je crois que je vais danser!'

And spreading out her dress, she chasséed across the room; till having reached Mr Rochester, she wheeled lightly round before him on tip-toe, then dropped on one knee at his feet, exclaiming: –

'Monsieur, je vous remercie mille fois de votre bonté;' then rising, she added, 'C'est comme cela que maman faisait, n'est-ce pas, monsieur?'

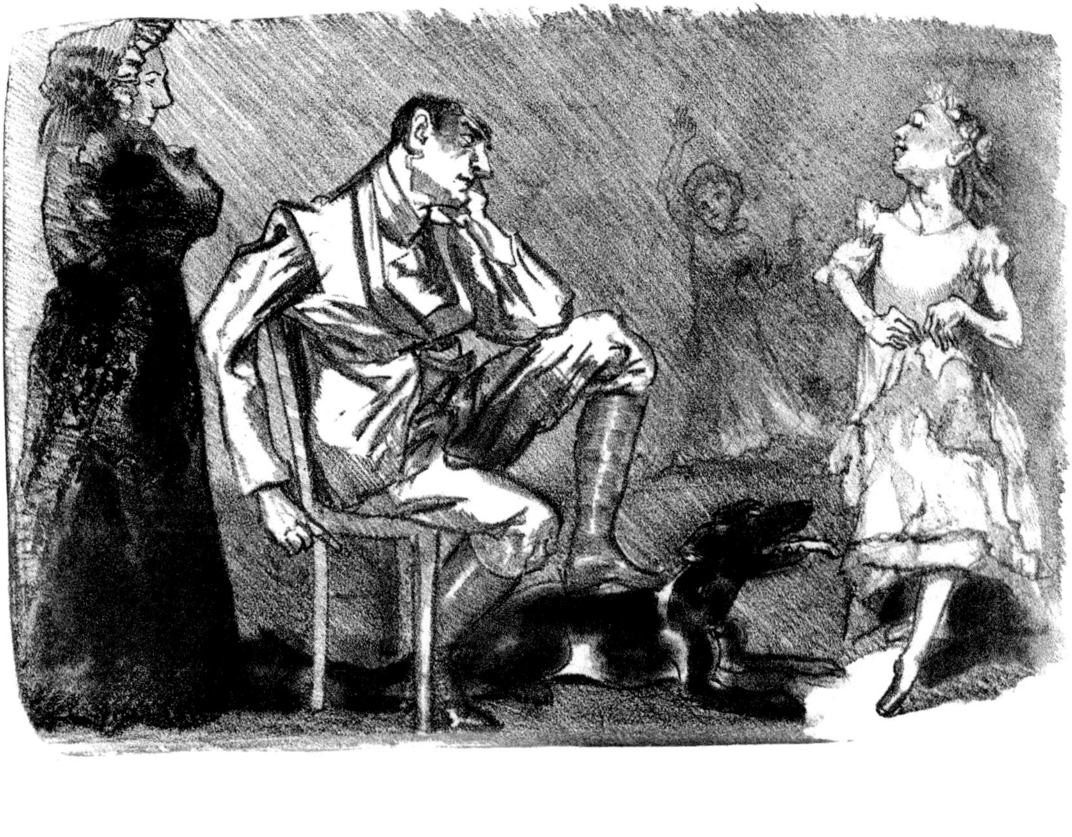

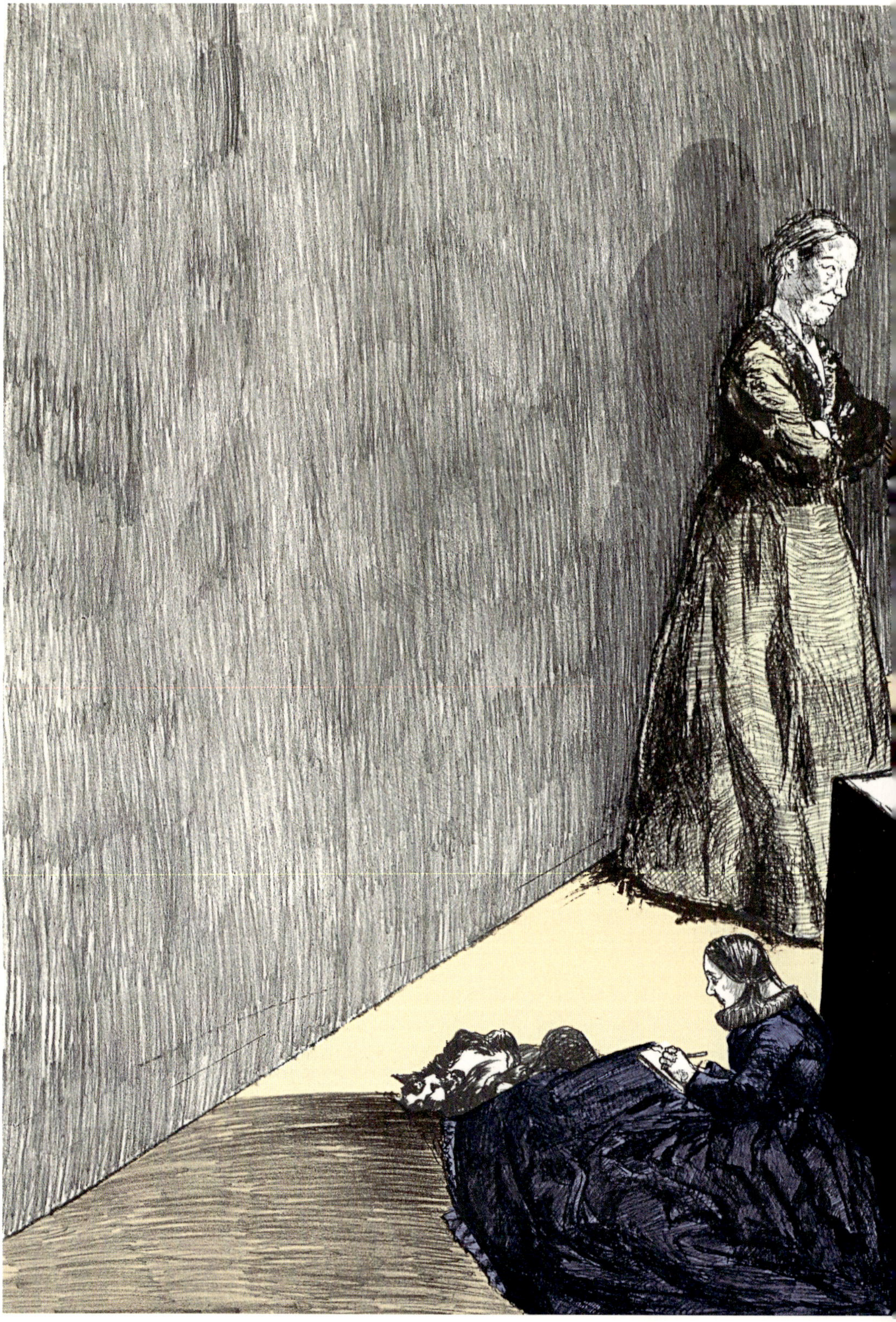

Getting Ready for the Ball

A JOYOUS STIR was now audible in the hall: gentlemen's deep tones, and ladies' silvery accents blent harmoniously together, and distinguishable above all, though not loud, was the sonorous voice of the master of Thornfield Hall, welcoming his fair and gallant guests under its roof. Then light steps ascended the stairs; and there was a tripping through the gallery, and soft, cheerful laughs, and opening and closing doors, and, for a time, a hush.

'Elles changent de toilettes,' said Adèle; who, listening attentively, had followed every movement; and she sighed.

'Chez maman,' said she, 'quand il y avait du monde, je les suivais partout, au salon et à leurs chambres; souvent je regardais les femmes de chambre coiffer et habiller les dames, et c'était si amusant: comme cela on apprend.'

*

Presently the chambers gave up their fair tenants one after another: each came out gaily and airily, with dress that gleamed lustrous through the dusk. For a moment they stood grouped together at the other extremity of the gallery, conversing in a key of sweet subdued vivacity: they then descended the staircase almost as noiselessly as a bright mist rolls down a hill. Their collective appearance had left on me an impression of high-born elegance, such as I had never before received.

I found Adèle peeping through the school-room door, which she held ajar. 'What beautiful ladies!' cried she in English. 'Oh, I wish I might go to them! Do you think Mr Rochester will send for us by-and-by, after dinner?'

'No, indeed, I don't; Mr Rochester has something else to think about. Never mind the ladies to-night; perhaps you will see them to-morrow: here is your dinner.'

Self Portrait with Grandchildren

YOU ARE NOT to suppose, reader, that Adèle has all this time been sitting motionless on the stool at my feet: no; when the ladies entered, she rose, advanced to meet them, made a stately reverence, and said, with gravity, –

'Bon jour, mesdames.'

And Miss Ingram had looked down at her with a mocking air, and exclaimed, 'Oh, what a little puppet!'

Lady Lynn had remarked, 'It is Mr Rochester's ward, I suppose – the little French girl he was speaking of.'

Mrs Dent had kindly taken her hand, and given her a kiss. Amy and Louisa Eshton had cried out simultaneously, –

'What a love of a child!'

And then they had called her to a sofa, where she now sat, ensconced between them, chattering alternately in French and broken English; absorbing not only the young ladies' attention, but that of Mrs Eshton and Lady Lynn, and getting spoilt to her heart's content.

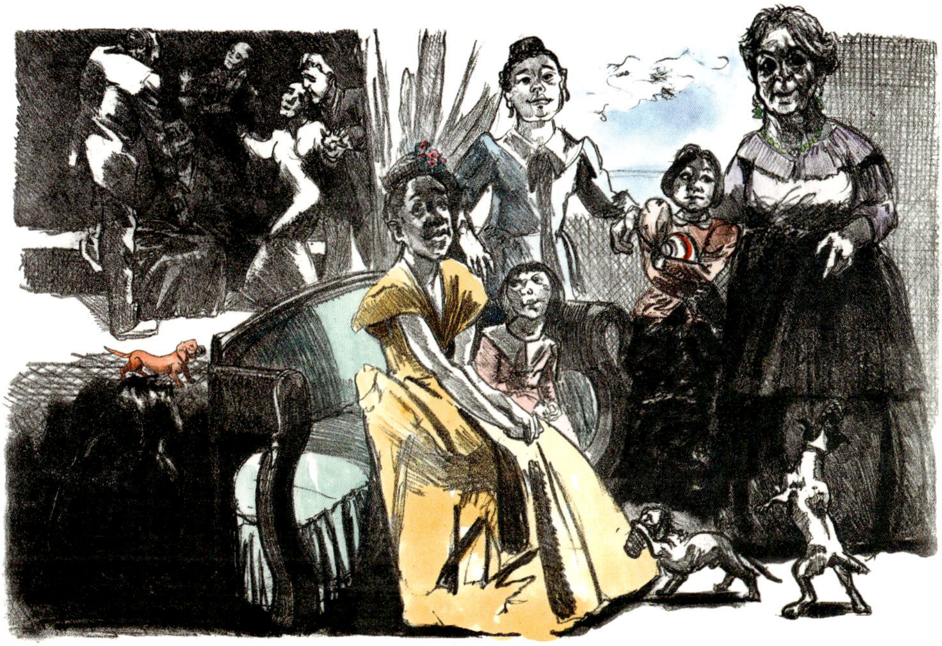

Dressing him up as Bluebeard

Seated on the carpet, by the side of this basin, was seen Mr Rochester, costumed in shawls, with a turban on his head. His dark eyes and swarth skin and Paynim features suited the costume exactly: he looked the very model of an eastern emir; an agent or a victim of the bowstring.

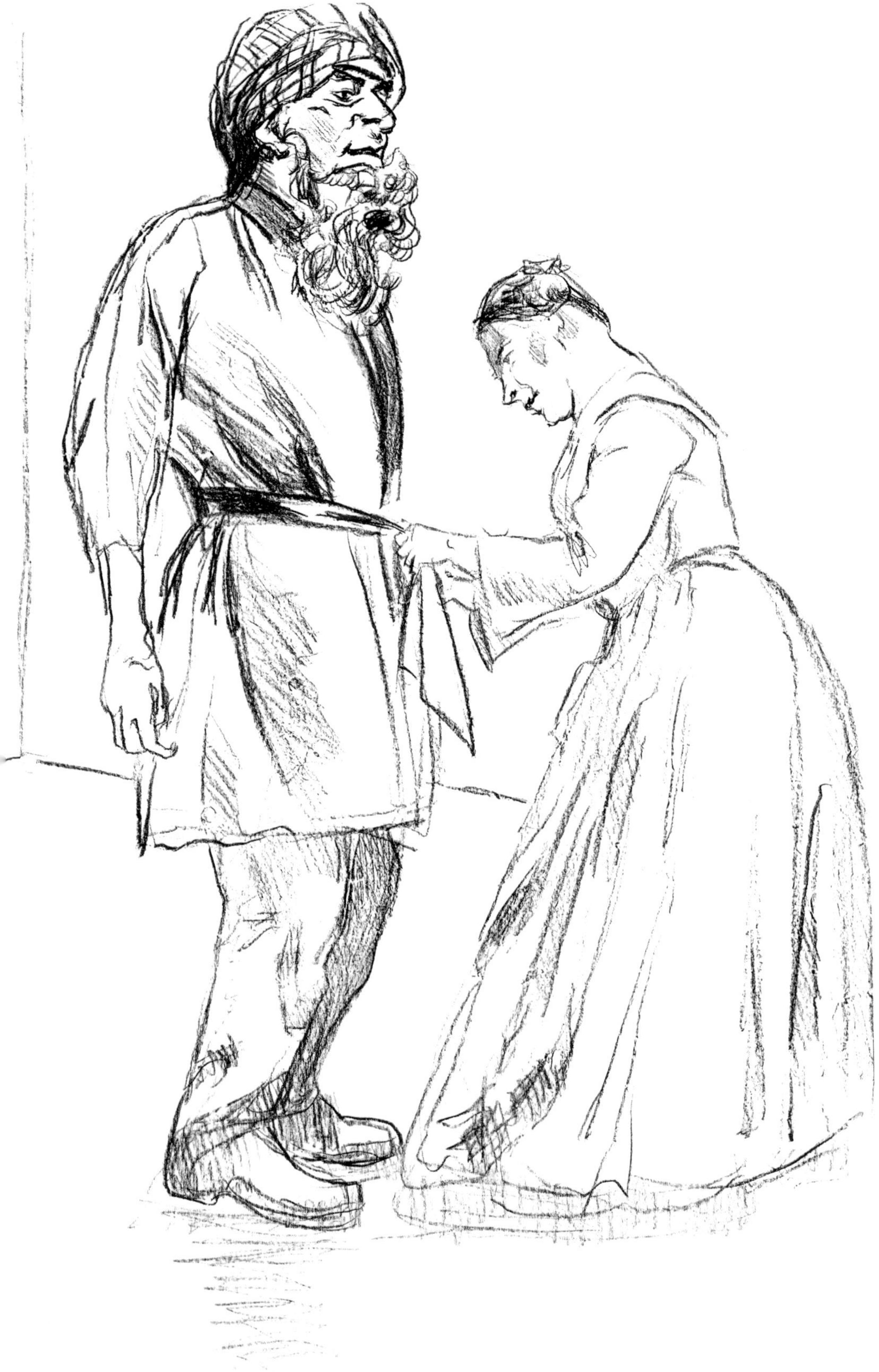

Biting

'She bit me,' he murmured. 'She worried me like a tigress, when Rochester got the knife from her.'

'You should not have yielded: you should have grappled with her at once,' said Mr Rochester.

'But under such circumstances, what could one do?' returned Mason. 'Oh, it was frightful!' he added, shuddering. 'And I did not expect it: she looked so quiet at first.'

'I warned you,' was his friend's answer; 'I said – be on your guard when you go near her. Besides, you might have waited till tomorrow, and had me with you: it was mere folly to attempt the interview to-night, and alone.'

'I thought I could have done some good.'

'You thought! you thought! Yes; it makes me impatient to hear you: but, however, you have suffered, and are likely to suffer enough for not taking my advice; so I'll say no more. Carter – hurry! – hurry! The sun will soon rise, and I must have him off.'

'Directly, sir; the shoulder is just bandaged. I must look to this other wound in the arm: she has had her teeth here too, I think.'

'She sucked the blood: she said she'd drain my heart,' said Mason.

I saw Mr Rochester shudder: a singularly marked expression of disgust, horror, hatred, warped his countenance almost to distortion; but he only said: –

'Come, be silent, Richard, and never mind her gibberish: don't repeat it.'

'I wish I could forget it,' was the answer.

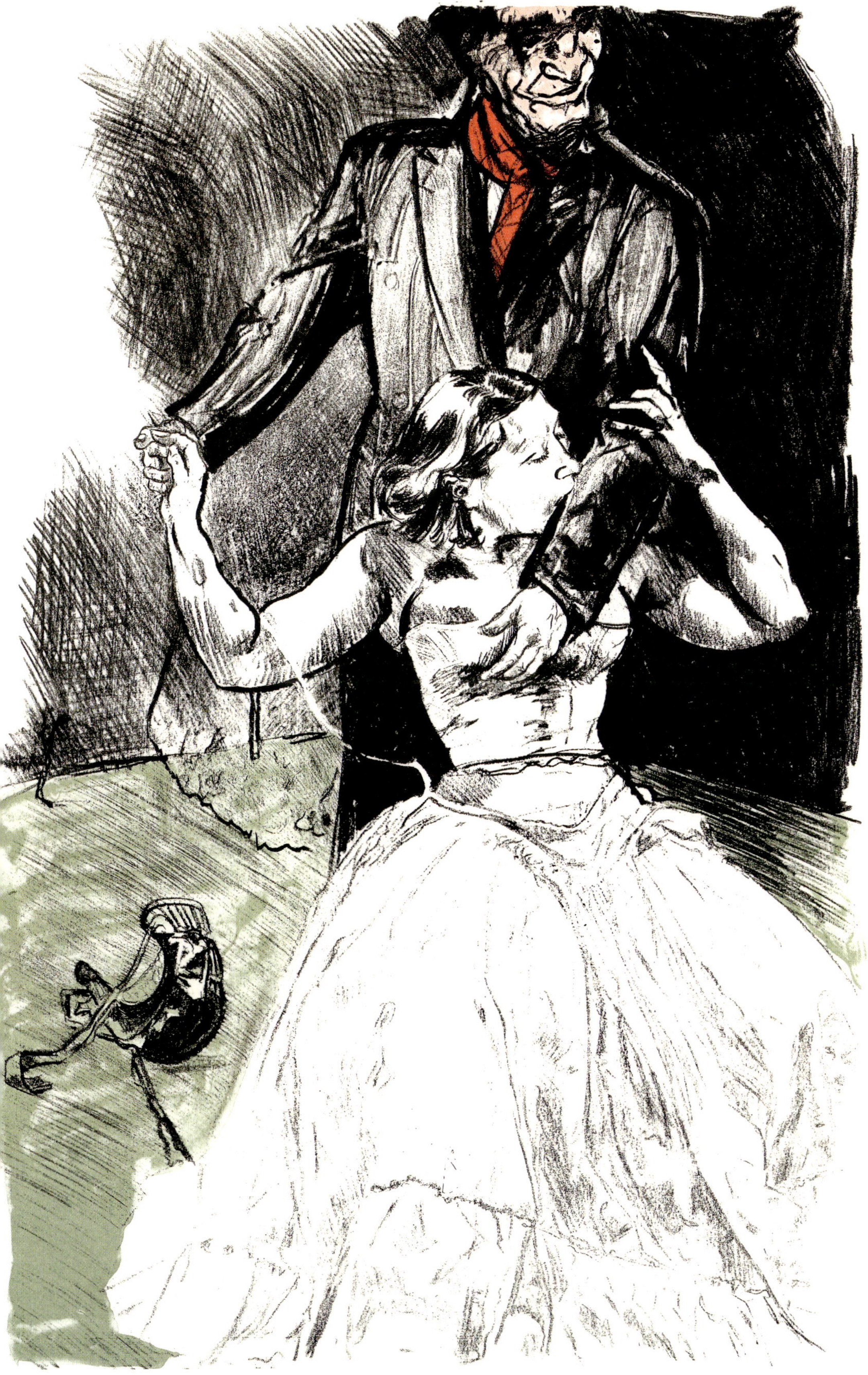

Up the Tree

IT WAS NOT without a certain wild pleasure I ran before the wind delivering my trouble of mind to the measureless air-torrent thundering through space. Descending the laurel-walk, I faced the wreck of the chestnut tree; it stood up, black and riven: the trunk, split down the centre, gaped ghastly. The cloven halves were not broken from each other, for the firm base and strong roots kept them unsundered below; though community of vitality was destroyed – the sap could flow no more: their great boughs on each side were dead, and next winter's tempests would be sure to fell one or both, to earth: as yet, however, they might be said to form one tree – a ruin; but an entire ruin.

'You did right to hold fast to each other,' I said: as if the monster-splinters were living things, and could hear me. 'I think, scathed as you look, and charred and scorched, there must be a little sense of life in you yet; rising out of that adhesion at the faithful, honest roots: you will never have green leaves more – never more see birds making nests and singing idyls in your boughs; the time of pleasure and love is over with you; but you are not desolate: each of you has a comrade to sympathize with him in his decay.' As I looked up at them, the moon appeared momentarily in that part of the sky which filled their fissure; her disk was blood-red and half overcast; she seemed to throw on me one bewildered, dreary glance, and buried herself again instantly in the deep drift of cloud. The wind fell, for a second, round Thornfield; but far away over wood and water, poured a wild, melancholy wail: it was sad to listen to, and I ran off again.

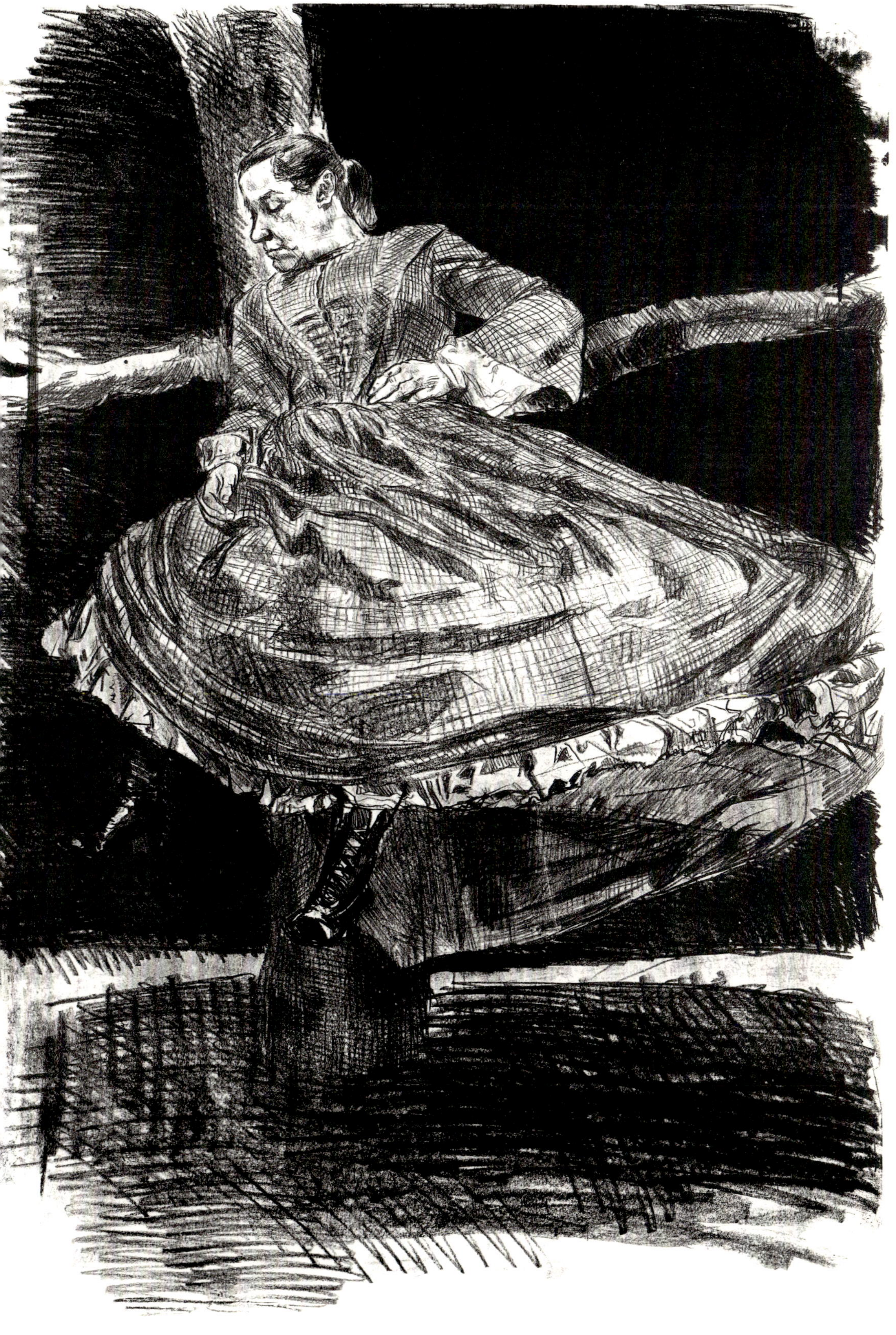

Crying

MY EYES WERE covered and closed: eddying darkness seemed to swim round me, and reflection came in as black and confused a flow. Self-abandoned, relaxed, and effortless, I seemed to have laid me down in the dried-up bed of a great river; I heard a flood loosened in remote mountains, and felt the torrent come: to rise I had no will, to flee I had no strength. I lay faint; longing to be dead. One idea only still throbbed life-like within me – a remembrance of God: it begot an unuttered prayer: these words went wandering up and down in my rayless mind, as something that should be whispered; but no energy was found to express them: –

'Be not far from me, for trouble is near: there is none to help.'

It was near: and as I had lifted no petition to Heaven to avert it – as I had neither joined my hands, nor bent my knees, nor moved my lips – it came: in full, heavy swing the torrent poured over me. The whole consciousness of my life lorn, my love lost, my hope quenched, my faith death-struck, swayed full and mighty above me in one sullen mass. That bitter hour cannot be described: in truth, 'the waters came into my soul; I sank in deep mire: I felt no standing; I came into deep waters; the floods overflowed me.'

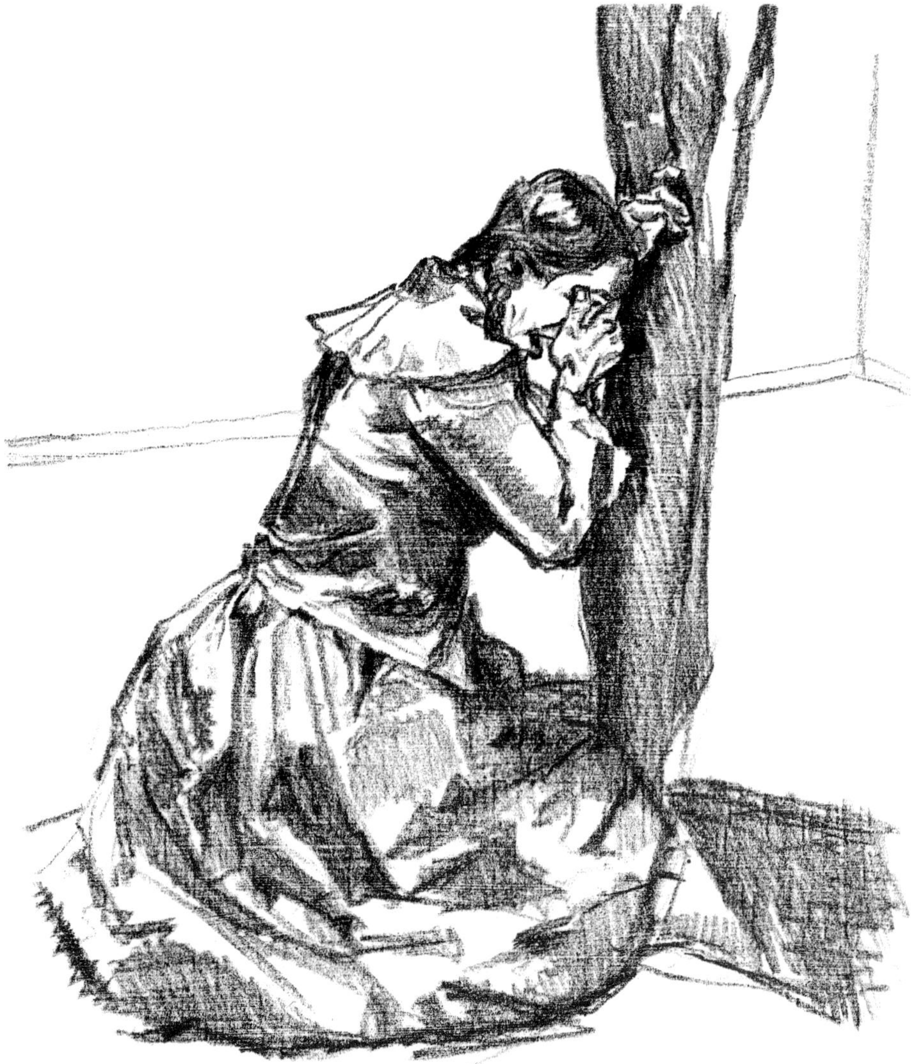

Bertha

'I LIVED WITH that woman upstairs four years, and before that time she had tried me indeed: her character ripened and developed with frightful rapidity; her vices sprang up fast and rank: they were so strong, only cruelty could check them; and I would not use cruelty. What a pigmy intellect she had – and what giant propensities! How fearful were the curses those propensities entailed on me! Bertha Mason, – the true daughter of an infamous mother, – dragged me through all the hideous and degrading agonies which must attend a man bound to a wife at once intemperate and unchaste.

'My brother in the interval was dead; and at the end of the four years my father died too. I was rich enough now – yet poor to hideous indigence: a nature the most gross, impure, depraved I ever saw, was associated with mine, and called by the law and by society a part of me. And I could not rid myself of it by any legal proceedings: for the doctors now discovered that *my wife* was mad – her excesses had prematurely developed the germs of insanity.'

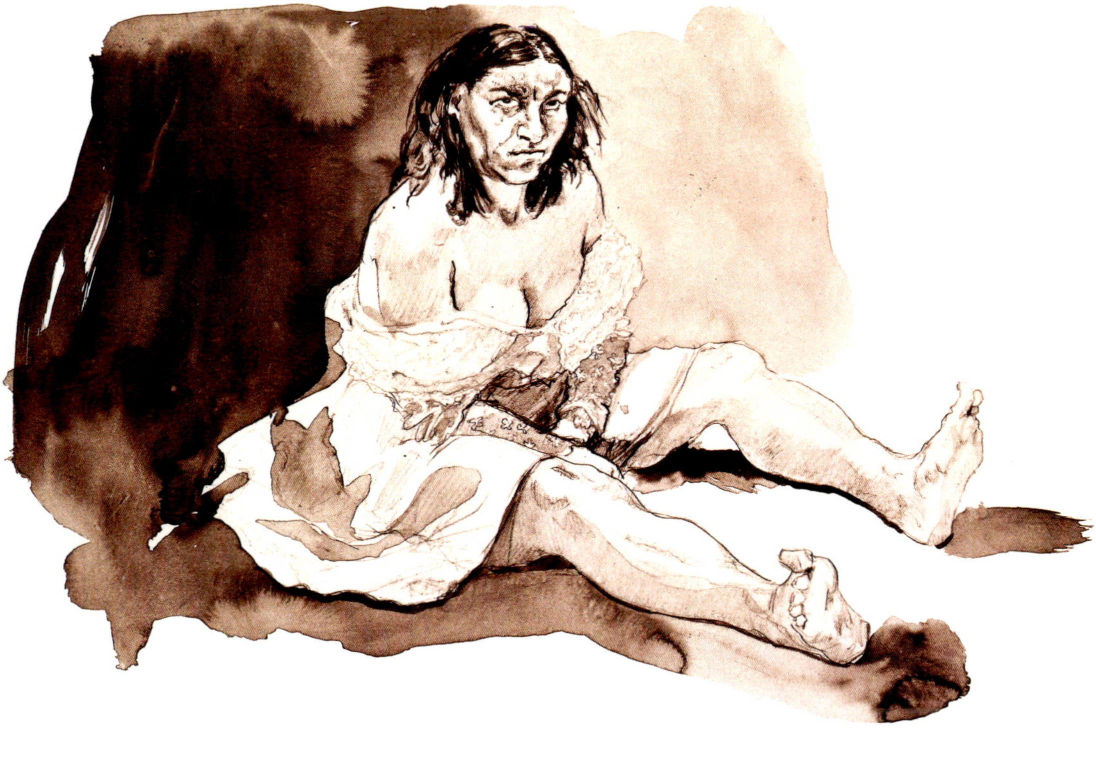

The Keeper

'To England, then, I conveyed her; a fearful voyage I had with such a monster in the vessel. Glad was I when I at last got her to Thornfield, and saw her safely lodged in that third story room, of whose secret inner cabinet she has now for ten years made a wild beast's den – a goblin's cell. I had some trouble in finding an attendant for her: as it was necessary to select one on whose fidelity dependence could be placed; for her ravings would inevitably betray my secret: besides, she had lucid intervals of days – sometimes weeks – which she filled up with abuse of me. At last I hired Grace Poole, from the Grimsby Retreat. She and the surgeon, Carter (who dressed Mason's wounds that night he was stabbed and worried), are the only two I have ever admitted to my confidence. Mrs Fairfax may indeed have suspected something; but she could have gained no precise knowledge as to facts. Grace has, on the whole, proved a good keeper: though, owing partly to a fault of her own, of which it appears nothing can cure her, and which is incident to her harassing profession, her vigilance has been more than once lulled and baffled. The lunatic is both cunning and malignant.'

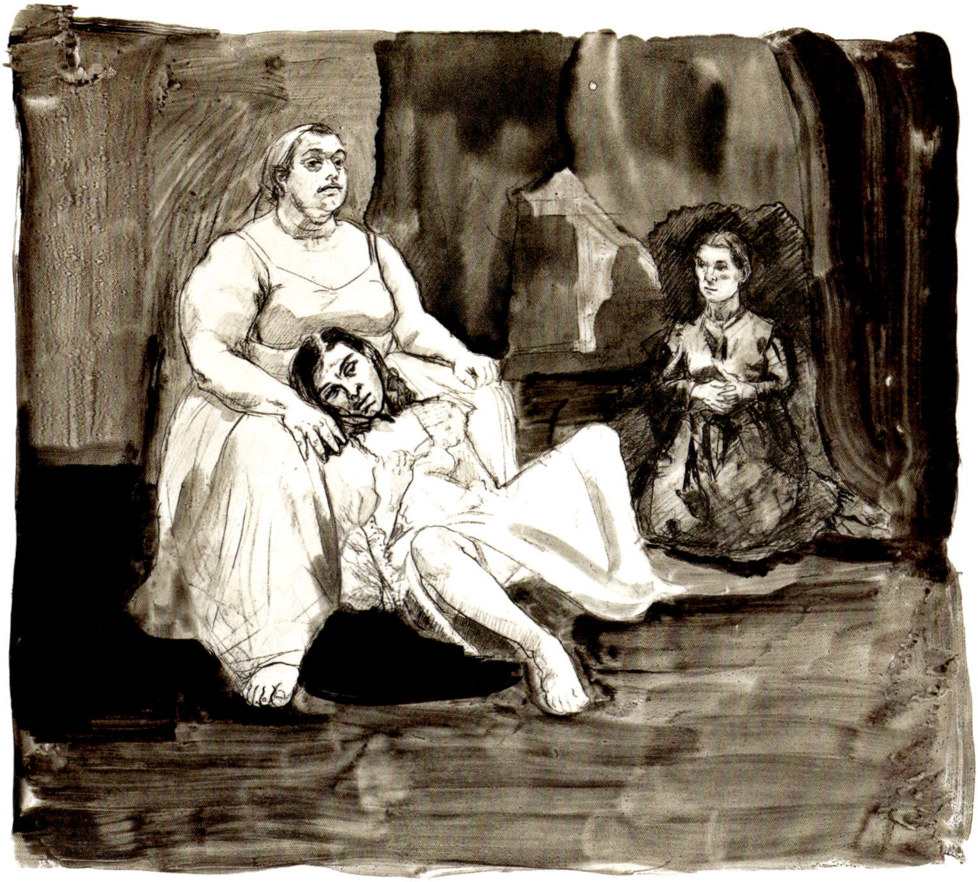

Undressing

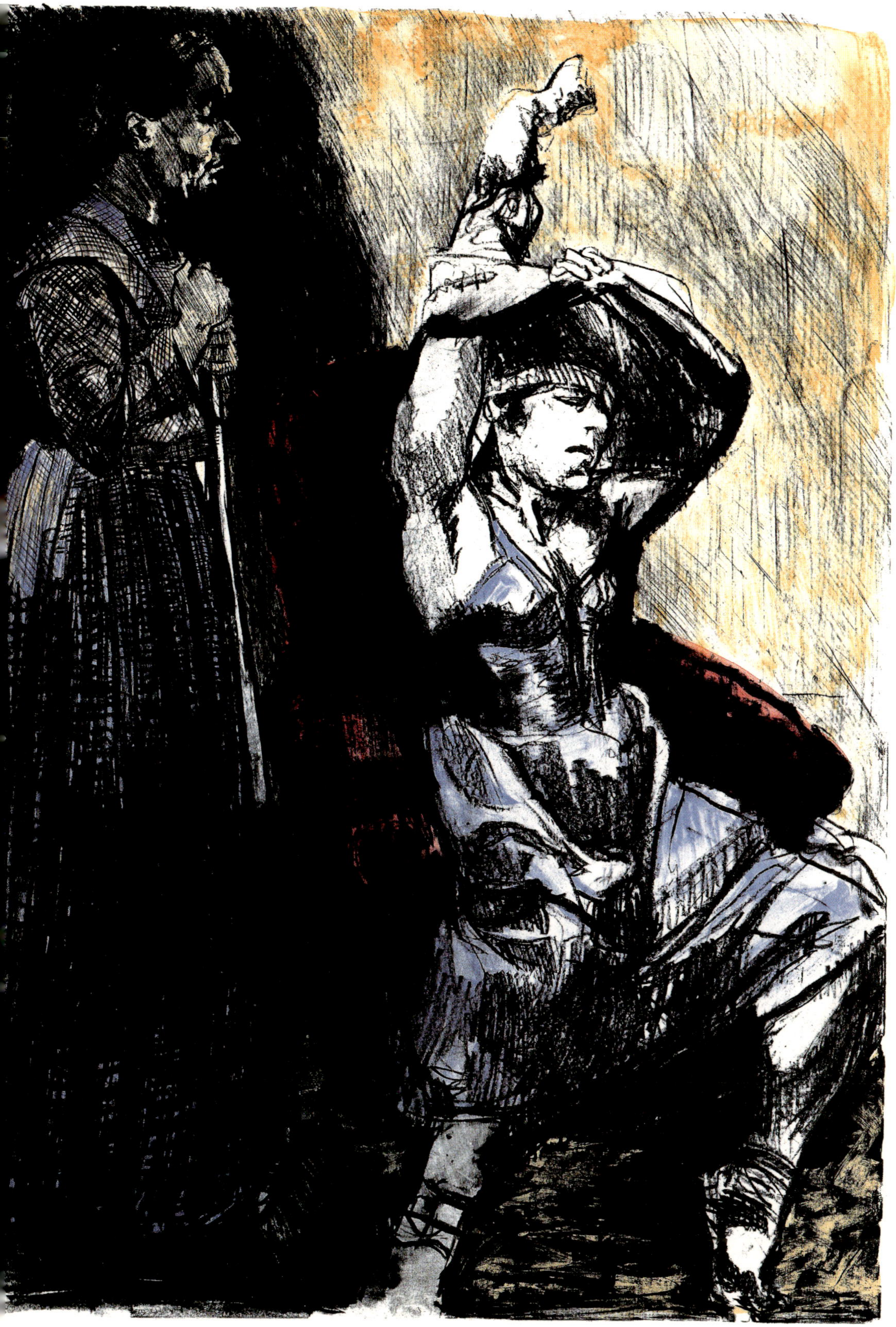

Night

DREARILY I WOUND my way down stairs: I knew what I had to do, and I did it mechanically. I sought the key of the side-door in the kitchen; I sought, too, a phial of oil and a feather; I oiled the key and the lock. I got some water, I got some bread: for perhaps I should have to walk far; and my strength, sorely shaken of late, must not break down. All this I did without one sound. I opened the door, passed out, shut it softly. Dim dawn glimmered in the yard. The great gates were closed and locked; but a wicket in one of them was only latched. Through that I departed: it, too, I shut; and now I was out of Thornfield.

A mile off, beyond the fields, lay a road which stretched in the contrary direction to Millcote; a road I had never travelled, but often noticed, and wondered where it led: thither I bent my steps. No reflection was to be allowed now: not one glance was to be cast back; not even one forward. Not one thought was to be given either to the past or the future. The first was a page so heavenly sweet – so deadly sad – that to read one line of it would dissolve my courage and break down my energy. The last was an awful blank: something like the world when the deluge was gone by.

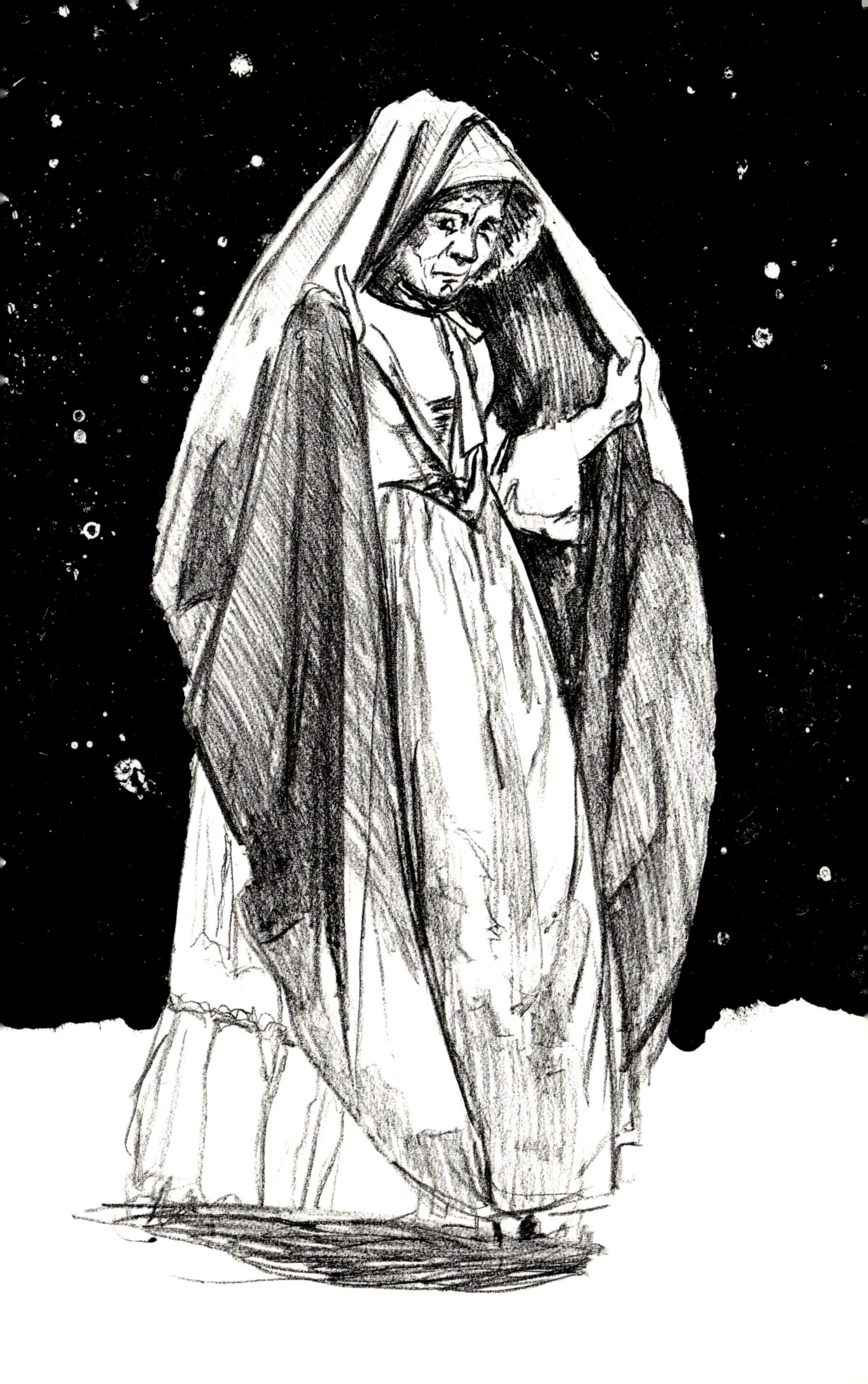

Come to Me

ALL THE HOUSE was still; for I believe all, except St John and myself, were now retired to rest. The one candle was dying out: the room was full of moonlight. My heart beat fast and thick: I heard its throb. Suddenly it stood still to an inexpressible feeling that thrilled it through, and passed at once to my head and extremities. The feeling was not like an electric shock; but it was quite as sharp, as strange, as startling: it acted on my senses as if their utmost activity hitherto had been but torpor; from which they were now summoned, and forced to wake. They rose expectant: eye and ear waited, while the flesh quivered on my bones.

'What have you heard? What do you see?' asked St John. I saw nothing: but I heard a voice somewhere cry –

'Jane! Jane! Jane!' nothing more.

'O God! what is it?' I gasped.

I might have said, 'Where is it?' for it did not seem in the room – nor in the house – nor in the garden: it did not come out of the air – nor from under the earth – nor from overhead. I had heard it – where, or whence, for ever impossible to know! And it was the voice of a human being – a known, loved, well-remembered voice – that of Edward Fairfax Rochester; and it spoke in pain and woe wildly, eerily, urgently.

'I am coming!' I cried. 'Wait for me! Oh, I will come!'

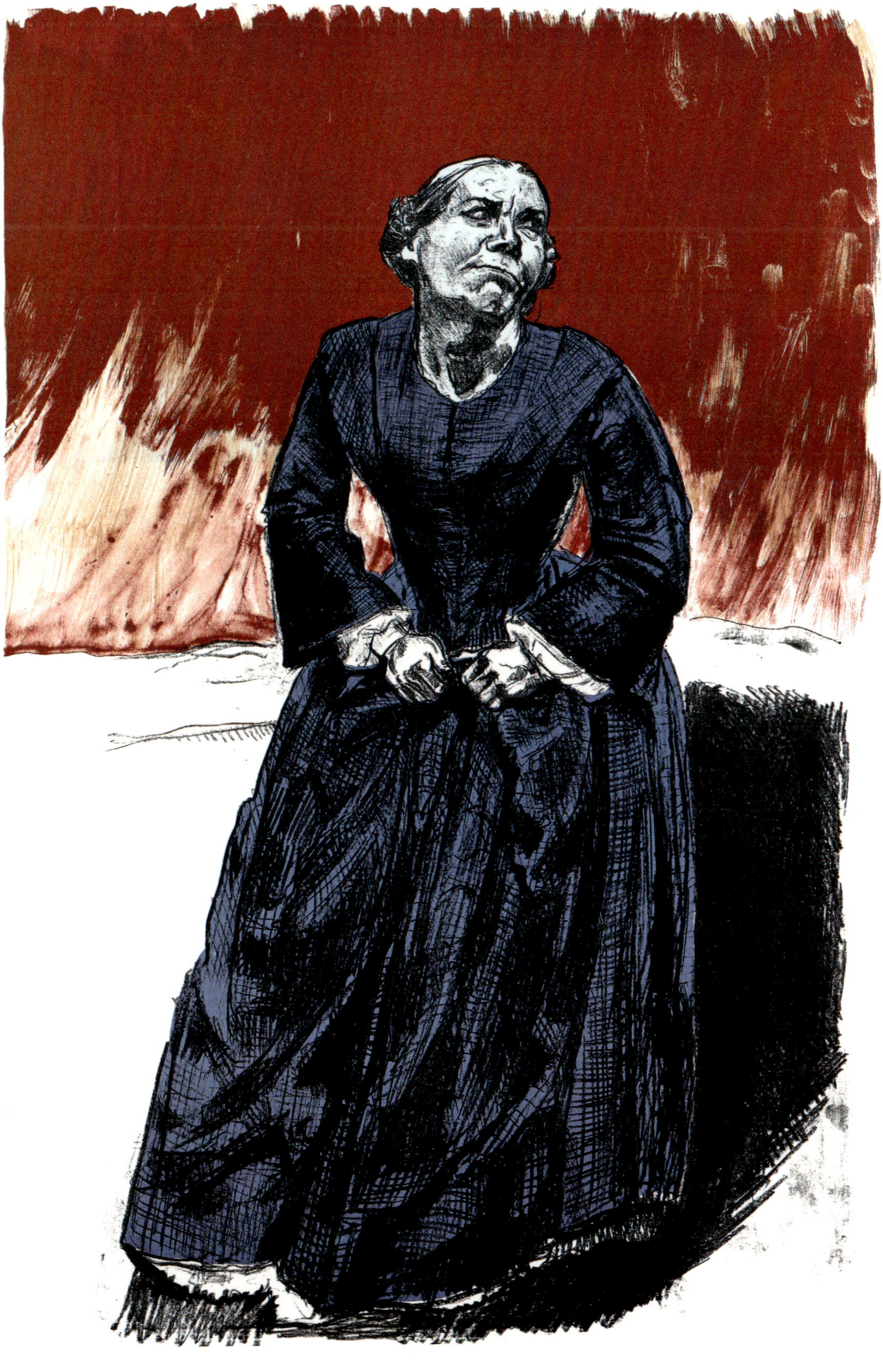

Jane Eyre has been designed by Peter B. Willberg
and printed and bound by Editoriale Bortolazzi Stei, Verona.
It is set in Monotype Janson and printed on 150gsm GardaPat,
with Flora Rustica endpapers.

It was originally published by Enitharmon Editions
as a signed and numbered artist's book
in an edition of seventy-five *de luxe* copies and
three hundred and fifty regular copies.